the DAILY FAMILY Conversation Starter

365 WAYS TO NURTURE CONNECTION, iNSPiRE PLAY, AND EMPOWER YOUR KiDS

Katie Clemons

HARPER
Celebrate

Published in Nashville, Tennessee, by Harper Celebrate, an imprint of HarperCollins Focus LLC.

Any internet addresses (websites, blogs, etc.) in this book are offered as a resource. They are not intended in any way to be or imply an endorsement by HarperCollins Focus LLC, nor does HarperCollins Focus LLC vouch for the content of these sites for the life of this book.

illustrations © Creative Market / RedChocolate
illustrations © Nicky Laatz
illustrations © iStockphoto / Andymo, Bubaone, Appleuzr, Olga Ubirailo, Sudowoodo, & Miray Celebi Kaba
Cover & interior design: Kathy Mitchell

ISBN 978-1-4002-4829-2 (epub)

ISBN 978-1-4002-4746-2 (TP)

Printed in Malaysia

24 25 26 27 28 VIV 5 4 3 2 1

To my wildly creative, brave, and kind little clan.
Charlotte, Linden, Amelia, and Niklas,
your stories are my favorite stories.

BECAUSE CONNECTION MATTERS: AN INTRODUCTION

Warm food spread across the kitchen counters. Loud, fast-paced conversation among my family members. To be honest, I can't actually recall a single word that was said. All these years later, all I remember is the joy that radiated from my ninety-seven-year-old grandma's face.

"So what do you think?" someone asked my grandma.

She kept smiling. Then she looked down and scooped another bite of pumpkin pie into her mouth.

"Mom?" my dad asked.

We all kept watching her and waiting; she kept smiling, kept chewing.

My mom touched her arm gently, and my grandma looked over in surprise. She swallowed her pie, set down her fork, and reached for her ears. One at a time, she turned on her hearing aids.

Throughout the entire meal, my grandma hadn't heard a word of our conversation!

Her joy had nothing to do with the words and ideas buzzing around her. Her smile came simply from being surrounded by her family as we connected with each other.

Your family and mine all lead such busy lives, and it's often hard to find opportunities to sit down together as a family. Life becomes too busy, too frantic, too exhausting, and we overlook everyday moments of connection. We miss seeing that the people who gather around us are amazing.

Now that I'm a mom of four, I've learned that great day-to-day dialogue like I grew up with takes a lot of practice. If I ask, "How was your day?" my kids don't launch into an in-depth monologue while I listen and nod. No, they grunt "good" or shrug and say "fine" as they wander into another room. I know I'm not alone in this struggle to engage. So many families lack the space or the habit or the right circumstance for open dialogue that nurtures and engages everyone in the family.

Yet often all it takes is five minutes to change everything.

That's where this book comes in. Think of these pages as a map for guiding you through stimulating conversations. You'll explore serious and silly topics. You'll crack jokes, solve puzzles, and ask "what if?" You'll discuss topics like gratitude, failure, and a growth mindset. You'll learn about your family's past and daydream about the future. And, best of all, you'll feel confident being exactly who you are, surrounded by people who love you most.

When my family sits down for dinner or begins chatting during the pockets of our day, my toddler, Charlotte, can't fully understand what's being said. But I see her smile. She looks exactly like my grandma did, blissful because she knows one thing for certain:

There's nowhere else she'd rather be than at this spot and in this moment with the greatest treasure in life . . . her family.

You decide where this book will take you. To spur your family along the trail, I've included five guideposts to help you get the most from this yearlong journey into better conversation and everyday moments of connection. You may just find your greatest treasure has been right here all along.

STORYCATCHING GUIDEPOSTS: HOW TO USE THIS BOOK

The most meaningful connections in our lives are all about story. When you tell your stories, you open up space for others to tell theirs. You fall deeper in love with your family for who they are and the journey they've each taken. Each connection point that you share—from major milestones to a silly story or a quick T. rex hug (#238)—is like a twig or a bit of clay or plant matter that a bird adds to its nest. I call the act of collecting these precious moments "storycatching": a chance to create space to "catch" each other's stories. To listen. To show. To say, "Hey, you matter to me."

These five guideposts will help make your storycatching feel easy and fun.

1. USE THiS BOOK YOUR WAY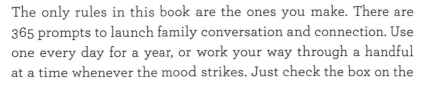

The only rules in this book are the ones you make. There are 365 prompts to launch family conversation and connection. Use one every day for a year, or work your way through a handful at a time whenever the mood strikes. Just check the box on the upper right of each prompt as you complete it. Begin with the first page, or jump around to prompts that intrigue you in the moment. Answer questions during commutes together, at the dinner table, before bed, or whenever you have a few minutes to chat and connect. You'll love what you discover about each other—and yourself!

2. SHARE YOUR STORIES

Are you ready to become a *raconteur*?

RACONTEUR

(rak-uhn-TUR), *noun*

someone who tells good stories

Becoming a great storyteller isn't as difficult as you might think! Don't worry if you think you aren't funny, you feel rambly, or you doubt you have all the answers. Sometimes you might not even remember all the details—and that's okay! Your story doesn't have to be perfect to be valuable, especially to your family.

I'll bet that more than anything, your family just wants to know you better.

3. Listen to Each Other

The conversation starters in this book give you an opportunity to peek inside one another's hearts and heads. Sometimes you'll hear things you already know about someone. Other times, you might discover details, emotions, or entire stories you weren't aware of!

Be patient. You might feel tempted to interrupt and jump in with your own story. Or maybe you feel a need to correct the storyteller or fix a problem for them. Instead, pause first.

More than anything, each member of your family needs to be heard. Does it really matter if a few details get jumbled up? Or if someone can't remember the right word for something? Listening well is one of the most powerful ways to communicate that you love someone.

4. Create a Five-Minute Habit

I'll bet your family's life is like mine, packed with an infinite number of activities to attend, chores to complete, and tasks to manage. It can be easy for a new routine to get lost in the shuffle, regardless of how important it is to you!

Try this:

Don't wait for the perfect date to start this book. Today is perfect! Turn to page 11: Conversation Guidelines. Talk through it as a family. Then set a goal to open this book at the same time every day for fourteen days. That's just two weeks of gifting yourselves five daily minutes to chat and play together. During that time, you'll see what works well for your family and what needs to change. Then revisit your family's guidelines, make necessary changes, and keep on storycatching!

5. GO BEYOND THESE PAGES

Visit my website for more story-prompting tools and ideas. My kids and I love playing these printable games, organizing family drawing challenges, and creating lunchbox notes together. They're all free and available to download at my website:

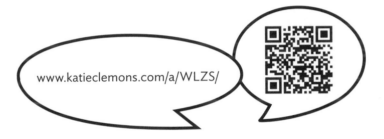

www.katieclemons.com/a/WLZS/

Thanks for inviting this book and me on your family journey. Write to me anytime at **howdy@katieclemons.com**, or tag me on social media **@katierclemons**, **#katieclemonsbooks**, and **#thedailyfamilyconvo**.

Now let's start talking and celebrate your story!

♡ Katie

CONVERSATION GUIDELINES

Let's switch things up! Raise your hand if you think kids should be in charge more often. Keep your hand up if you think kids should be the boss of this page. *POOF!*

HERE'S WHAT YOU'VE GOT TO DECIDE, BOSS:

Does the whole family have to be present to use this book?

Can other people join the conversation sometimes?

How many conversation starters can be used in one day?

Who's in charge of reading the conversation starters aloud?

Do we work through this book sequentially or turn to any page?

What will we be doing while we chat?

- ♡ eating dinner
- ♡ riding the subway or bus
- ♡ waiting at appointments
- ♡ sitting in the car
- ♡ snuggling before bed
- ♡ _____

WRITE YOUR NAME

Your signature is one way you make a mark on the world. No one writes your name quite like you. It's unique and special.

Sign your name on this page. Add your age too!

What do you like about your signature? Does it say something about you? Is it silly or serious, detailed or uncomplicated?

(Psst. Have a family member who can't write yet? Invite them to add a little scribble, or you can write their name for them.)

2

LOOKING BACK

What's something really wonderful that happened in your family last year? How does it feel to look back on this moment?

Listen to each other's memories. Sometimes other people cherish particular moments that you may have forgotten about or never even noticed.

Done ☐

3

HUH?

This one's just for kids:

List a few things grown-ups do that don't make sense.

DINNER POLL

What's your family's go-to weekend dinner like right now?

THIS? OR THAT?

Sit down together	Grab-and-go
At a restaurant	At home
Technology at the table	Unplugged
Meat-based	Vegetarian
Made from scratch	Quick and easy
TV on	TV off
Loads of veggies	No veggies
Fast	Slow
Dessert	Skip the dessert

Why do you think these choices are important for your family's current lifestyle?

BRAINSTORM

Brainstorming is a creative way to approach a challenge.
The rules are simple:

1 Think of lots of ideas.

2 Don't criticize anyone else's suggestions
or lack of suggestions.

3 Encourage every thought, even the crazy ones.

4 Ask "What if . . . ?"

5 Listen.

You're going to love all the brainstorming you'll be doing
together in this book. Sometimes it will be serious.
Sometimes it will be silly.

For instance, work together to brainstorm a solution to this
problem: A butterfly is trapped in your bedroom.
How can you help it get back outside?

MORE AND LESS

Knowing what your family wants more of and less of can help you understand each other better, and it makes being together more fun! When you know what makes your family happier—such as giving high fives or watching funny movies together—you can plan for more good stuff. Likewise, when you know what your family doesn't enjoy—such as teasing or seeing scary movies—you can be more conscious of each other's feelings and your own actions.

Brainstorm all the things your family wants more of and less of. Talk about why these things are important to you.

If you want, grab a sheet of paper and make a table like this one to jot down your ideas.

THIS YEAR, OUR FAMILY WOULD LIKE:

MORE OF THIS	LESS OF THIS

ROBOTIC

BEEP BOP BOOP BOOP.

Everyone talk like robots as you finish some of these sentences.
Hear how fun these ordinary topics become!

 One thing I need to do today is . . .

 One thing I'm eating a lot of today is . . .

FACTORY-MADE

Congratulations! If you love coming up with crazy ideas,
it's your lucky day.

Your family just inherited an abandoned factory and all the
money you need to make it operational again.
The only question is:

What do you want to produce in your new factory?

THE PERSON WHO TRIES

My dad was a lanky kid with glasses who wanted
to learn how to play American football.

"What position do you want?" the coach asked him.

My dad gulped and muttered the only position he knew:
"Um, lineman?"

A lineman, as you may know, is a football player known for
his sheer size and strength. He works with four other equally
powerful teammates to build an immense wall against the
opposing team's linemen. The whistle blows, and the linemen
charge each other in an attempt to break through
the others' wall.

My dad, however, was more of a slip-through-the-wall kind
of size. Game after game, he got flattened.

But he kept showing up. Deep inside, he had decided he would
be a person who tries.

TALK ABOUT THIS:

**Why do you think it's important to try new things,
even if it means you might get knocked down?**

NEW YEAR

How can you make this year better than last year?

LETTER ART

What do you see when you look at each of these boxes? They're not letters all jumbled up. They are the beginning of four doodles. Grab a pen and copy the drawing on a piece of paper and add as many details as you can imagine. Then talk about your new creations.

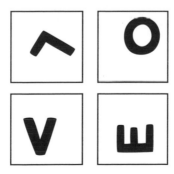

MOONWALK

ACT THiS OUT:

Your family's rocket just landed on the moon.
What a view! Everyone climb out of your spaceship
and walk around on the moon.

Remember: There's not much gravity, so you'll probably bounce
on each step. And bulky space suits don't make moving easy.
Try to give each other slow-motion high fives,
and communicate with radio voices.

SPAGHETTI

Which type of dish should people use to hold their spaghetti?

BOWL   PLATE

Why is your choice the best choice?

THAT'S ME!

Raise your hand if ...

You eat butter straight from the stick.

You jump in mud puddles.

You love dessert!

You sometimes pretend the floor is lava.

You have an idea for what your family should raise hands for next.

HEIRLOOMS

Heirlooms are precious keepsakes that have been handed down from generation to generation. Does your family own any heirlooms? Look at one and talk about its story.

LOVE NOTES

The way you speak to yourself is powerful. If you repeat uplifting messages and increase your positive self-talk, you'll nurture a can-do attitude deep inside.

Practice saying these messages out loud to yourself and your family:

Your kindness inspires people.

You have a bright and brilliant mind.

You are worthy of a great day today.

Your creativity knows no bounds.

You are surrounded by love.

You are loved just the way you are.

You are strong and resilient.

You are capable of achieving wonderful things.

(Take today's topic further by hanging little messages on the bathroom mirror, the fridge, the front door, or anywhere you and your family are sure to see them. Download ready-to-print love notes at www.katieclemons.com/a/JHKv/)

STITCHES

When you're a kid, you're bound to get in a few scrapes, and you might even need stitches. Stitches can be evidence of when you pushed boundaries, and they offer a chance to learn from mistakes and emerge stronger and ready for your next adventure.

TALK ABOUT THIS:

**When have you gotten stitches?
Do you still have the scar?**

BOREDOM

Ahh, boredom. It can feel like the exciting colors in your life have drained away. You want to feel motivated to jump up and do something, anything, but all you can see is black and white.

Talk about what boredom feels like to you. Then grab a sheet of paper and draw it.

19

DISCOVERY

Sometimes boredom catches you off guard. You've been so busy doing what other people planned or taking care of routine things like eating and getting dressed. Now there's nothing on your agenda.

Your brain is craving something. Hmm . . .

You go to an adult for ideas.
(Watch out! They might suggest chores!)

No, their ideas don't cure the restlessness you feel.
Keep letting your mind wander. An idea will come . . .

Eureka!

TALK ABOUT THIS:

What's an incredible discovery you've had or a project you've built after you felt bored?

Ask an adult to share something they did as a kid too.

WEIRD FOOD

Would you ever eat or drink these things?
Or have you already tried them?

Pickled pigs' feet

Frog legs

Fried butter

Clamato juice (tomato juice plus clam juice)

Oxtail soup

Chocolate-covered crickets

Lutefisk (codfish soaked in lye)

OUR LIST

Do you ever daydream about the things you'd like to do with your family? It's fun to imagine the experiences you want to share and things you might try. Sometimes your ideas might be really big. Other times, they're everyday moments.
They all matter.

Talk about some of the things you'd like to do with your family. Here are a few questions to help you brainstorm.

Where would you love to take a family vacation?

What's something you'd like to accomplish together?

Is there a restaurant or type of food that you'd like to try?

Is there a new activity you'd like to do?

What's a local activity that you'd like to try?

(Psst. Explore fun family ideas my kids and I have planned at www.katieclemons.com/a/dSpp/)

22

TWISTED TONGUE

What happens when your family tries to speak at lightning speed? Watch out! You might tangle your tongues with these tongue twisters. Try saying each one slowly, then go faster and faster.

A big bug bit the little beetle but the little beetle bit the big bug back.

If a dog chews shoes, whose shoes does he choose?

Top chopstick shops stock top chopsticks.

I saw a kitten eating chicken in the kitchen.

Done ☐

23

AWW, NUTS!

Talk about how everyone should pronounce *pecan*:

PEE-can   or   **puh-KHAN**

WE ARGUE

We all want to be right when we argue. The challenge is to remember that the person you're disagreeing with is probably more important to you than the satisfaction of being right.

Ask yourself: Do I care more about the problem or the other person?

Think back on a recent argument you had with a family member or a friend. Are there ways you could have changed your response to the situation by focusing more on the other person?

SMILE

EVERYONE TAKE A TURN FINISHING THIS SENTENCE ALOUD:

I smiled a lot today when _____ .

OUTSIDE AND INSIDE

Chat about things your family loves doing this time of year, both inside and out. Then jot some down in these columns.

OUTSIDE	INSIDE

BALANCE

Can you walk with a book balanced on your head? Take turns trying with books of different shapes and sizes. Who in your family can balance more than one?

28

FULL BOWL

If this bowl were in front of you right now,
what would you want it to be full of?

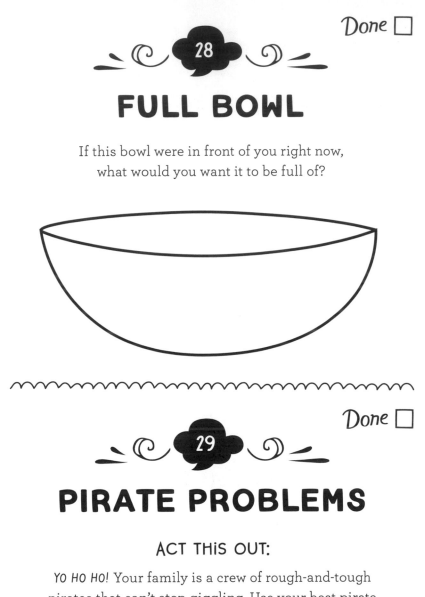

29

PIRATE PROBLEMS

ACT THiS OUT:

YO HO HO! Your family is a crew of rough-and-tough
pirates that can't stop giggling. Use your best pirate
voices to explain what's so funny.

30

THE DOORBELL

DING-DONG. KNOCK-KNOCK-KNOCK.

Someone is stopping by your home. Do they have a package?
Are they here to play? Something else? Chances are,
you know who's most likely to stop by.

Talk about who they are. How do you always know it's them?

31

HIP HIP HOORAY!

On a separate piece of paper, design a family pennant that
you'd love to wave when you celebrate and support each other.

You can write encouraging words like "Bravo!" and "You've
got this!" Add doodles, include your last name, or give it some
color—whatever you want to make it yours.

32

CELEBRATIONS

Sound the drums! Throw the confetti! It's time to celebrate some family milestones and adventures big and small.

Has someone in your family done any of these things over the past year? Color in each box that gets a yes, or mark each one with something small, like a coin or piece of candy.
Can you get four in a row? Or a blackout?

Got an award	Participated in a club	Went on a vacation	Kept a journal
Read a challenging book	Learned something new	Practiced a sport	Listened to live music
Rode on a bus	Visited the library	Rode a bike	Achieved something scary
Played an instrument	Made a new friend	Lost a tooth	Made something cool

ANSWER THAT

Asking questions is an important part of how we learn. It's how we gain more information about something and discover how to communicate with other people.

I wonder what happens when you have the answer but don't know the question. Today's conversation starters are a fun twist to find out.

1. The answer is: lemonade.

What's the question?

2. The answer is: five dollars.

What's the question?

3. The answer is: a pair of pants.

What's the question?

TECH-LESS

Interview the adults with you to learn more about when they were kids. Ask them these questions:

*If you wanted to meet up with a friend,
how did you make a plan?*

How did your parents know where you were?

How did you find your way to a new place?

35

WHY?

Why did this chicken cross this road?

BLUSTERY DAY

A blustery day can feel like a grumpy day. Cold wind howls in strong gusts, so it's not the greatest day for going outside.

Think of some things your family could do together on a blustery day, and discuss or make a list on a sheet of paper.

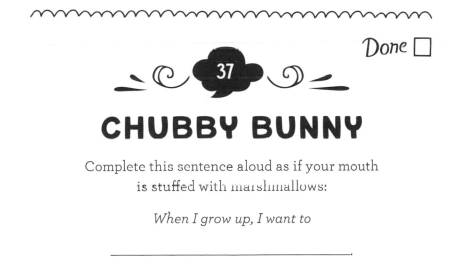

CHUBBY BUNNY

Complete this sentence aloud as if your mouth is stuffed with marshmallows:

When I grow up, I want to

_____.

Ask adults to try this sentence aloud:

When I was a kid, I wanted to grow up to

_____.

38

NOSE WORKOUT

Talk about which smell is better:

THIS? OR THAT?

Flowers	Pine trees
Vanilla	Peppermint
Beer	Coffee
Freshly-cut grass	Baking bread
Mouthwash	Bad breath
Strawberries	Oranges
Vinegar	Soy sauce

Done ☐

39

CHORES

What's one chore you actually enjoy doing?

MIRROR

Can you read this message aloud? It's difficult to do!

Our family
makes a lot of
mistakes. That's
okay.
It's how we
learn. Our
family has a lot
of fun!

Now try a cool trick. Stand in front of a mirror
and hold up this page. Now read the message aloud.

Do you think it's true?

CONFLICT

Conflict is a natural part of being in a family.

I remember a particular afternoon when my sister and I were kids. We were supposed to clean our bedroom, but we couldn't stop fighting. We bickered about who'd made which messes and which toys belonged to whom. I was in a hurry to get outside; she wanted to play as she went. We couldn't agree on anything! Everything was the other's fault. Smoke was blowing out our ears.

Sometimes it's not about being right or wrong. Sometimes we have to learn to work together.

My sister and I eventually divided up the tasks and got the job done.

I know it's not always easy. Your family is made up of all different people with unique ideas and emotions. But you're also a team.

TALK ABOUT THiS:

How can you use more kindness when you're working with your family on a chore or problem?

EMOJI FACE

Which emoji face are you today and why?

EVERYONE, TALK ABOUT iT, OR DRAW YOURS HERE:

DIVE IN

Imagine having your own private swimming pool. Pretty
awesome, right? If you could put anything you wanted inside
your pool, what would you fill it with?
The one thing you can't put in:

WATER

MOTHER EARTH

Many Native American religions believe Earth is mother to
all things. All plants and creatures depend on Earth for water,
food, clothing, and shelter. Often, we all get so busy thinking
about the things we want and need that we don't always think
about the best way to care for the planet.

WHAT DO YOU THINK?

**Does the Earth belong to people?
Or do people belong to the Earth?**

45

WUNDERKAMMER

A wunderkammer is a room or cabinet filled with rare and remarkable objects, such as animal skeletons, shells, minerals, books, art, and other interesting and worldly artifacts.

We all have our own treasure troves of weird and wonderful things that we've accumulated. Your collection might demonstrate things you've learned, milestones you've achieved, or places you've been.

TRY THIS:

Take a tour around your home to visit each other's collections. Pick one object from your collection and share a story about it.

CALMING

TRY THIS:

Lie down somewhere comfortable. Close your eyes gently, and let your arms and legs fall to your sides. Take in a long, slow breath. Be relaxed and calm. Breathe out, letting your thoughts drift away. Breathe in, noticing how your belly moves up. Now breathe out again, feeling your belly come back down. Breathe in. Breathe out.

Now shift your attention to your day. As you breathe in, think of something that went really well. Breathe out. Did it make you feel good? Breathe in. Did it make you feel proud? Breathe out. Keep breathing and thinking about your day.

When you're ready, open your eyes. You can keep lying down as you answer this question:

What made today a good day?

47

LOVE LETTER

Raise your hand if you're the youngest person here.

YAHOO! Your family needs the first letter of your name for today's conversation. Do you know what that letter is?

Everyone work together to find a word or phrase that fits each category below. Each answer must begin with that letter.

What can your family come up with together?

A bad choice for a pet

Something we shout

A part of the body

An ice cream flavor

A job

Something green

Something we do every day

Something we see right now

WALL TREASURE

Name a favorite thing that hangs on your wall.

~~~~~~~~~~~~~~~~~~~~~~~~~~~~~~~~~~

SEIZE THE DAY

CARPE DIEM!

This Latin phrase translates to "Seize the day!" It's a reminder to embrace opportunities in your life and make the most of every moment. How does your family seize the day?

Use this motto right now to capture some spontaneous, joyful selfies of you and your family. Pick one or try them all:

- ♡ Posing with water
- ♡ Hugging each other
- ♡ Pointing at something
- ♡ Having fake pouty faces
- ♡ Hiding behind books

COMFORT FOOD

Comfort food is any food that feels sentimental to you.
It's something that reminds you of home, a piece of your
childhood, a place you've been, or your culture.

Do you have a comfort food?

ASK THE ADULTS WiTH YOU:

Will you tell me about one of your favorite
comfort foods from childhood?

WORLD RENOWNED

TRUE OR FALSE?

Your life is easier when you're famous.

SOUNDS FUNNY

What's the funniest sound you can make? Try out a few.

When everyone's found a great sound, create a symphony.
Pick someone to be the conductor. Each time that person
points at you, make your sound. When the conductor points at
someone else, they make their sound. Your conductor can play
with different tempos and cadences. Get really quiet (it's called
pianissimo) or grow very loud (fortissimo).
What a beautiful racket!

GIFT

If you were to receive a present right now,
what would you like it to be?

Listen to what everyone else would wish for too.

TRACE OUR HANDS

On a separate piece of paper, have each family member trace their hands. Overlap handprints if needed.

While you trace, share some memories of when you were little and your hands were smaller. How does it feel to grow up?

FISH FACE

Think of one of your talents or hobbies that you're really proud of.

Now pretend you're a goldfish telling your family all about it. Open your mouth as big as you can for your first word. Then close your mouth. Then open it really big for the next word. Close it. And so on!

HERE'S A PROMPT TO GET YOU STARTED:

I love how I can _____ .

56

BE KIND, PLEASE REWIND

We couldn't stream videos when I was a kid. If we wanted to watch a new movie, my family rented a VHS tape at the grocery store.

These tapes were about the size of this book and contained one movie on a strip of tape between two reels. After you watched a movie, the tape had to be rewound back to the first reel before anyone could watch it again.

Many video rental shops put a neon sticker on every tape:

BE KIND, PLEASE REWIND

No one was required to rewind the tape. There wasn't a fine or punishment if you didn't do it. Rewinding the tape for the next renter was just a kind gesture.

Sometimes kindness doesn't come with a reward or thanks.

KEEP GOING

Do you ever do something simple and kind for other people?

How does it make you feel?

How do you think it makes the recipients feel?

~~~~~~

Done ☐

57

WHAT YOU REALLY NEED

Marcus Aurelius was a Roman emperor who ruled almost two thousand years ago. Back then, people didn't have access to most of the everyday things that are a normal part of your life. People couldn't eat unlimited bananas. There was no electricity to switch on a light. And yet Marcus Aurelius wrote:

"REMEMBER THIS, THAT VERY LITTLE IS NEEDED TO MAKE A HAPPY LIFE."

What are the things that make you happy?
Talk about them with your family.

FAUCET

Oh dear. Your family had to call a plumber to fix the kitchen faucet the other day. For whatever reason, the plumber failed to mention it was Wacky Wednesday, and now when you flip on the faucet, water doesn't pour out. Something else does.

 What kind of liquid would you like to have come out of your faucet?

FRIES WITH THAT?

TRUE OR FALSE?

There's just no point in eating french fries without ketchup.

Hey, have you ever tried fries with mayonnaise? It's a common dip in many European cultures.

YOU BETCHA!

Often people fall into a rhythm of saying the same things, and we forget the other really cool ways we could express ourselves.

When I was at the grocery store recently, I thanked the clerk for handing me my receipt.

"You betcha," she answered with a happy grin.

You betcha. What a breezy way to say you're welcome.

TALK ABOUT THIS:

What are some words or phrases that you think people should say more often?

ROCK STAR ☆

Pretend you're in a family rock band. Play the air guitar or beat the drums as you describe today's weather and how it impacted your day.

Done ☐

SUCCESSFUL

Does success have to mean you take home the first-place trophy? Or does success mean making progress so that you become better and better at what you do?

In everything you do, you'll have good days and bad days. Sometimes you'll achieve great things, and sometimes you won't. Do the bad days mean you quit trying, or do you dust yourself off, keep learning, and try again the next time?

Even the greatest athletes don't always win, and they dedicate their whole lives to their sport.
Not everyone gets the trophy every time.

TALK ABOUT THIS:

Do you need to win in order to be successful at something?

Done ☐

BEING BOSS

What would you change if you were the leader of the country? What would you fight to never change?

Done ☐

BENDY FACE

Is your face a bendy face? I cannot get the tip of my tongue to touch my nose, and I can't twist my tongue downward to touch my chin either. But some people can!

Can any of you?

TRY THESE:

1 Touch your nose with the tip of your tongue.

2 Touch your chin with the tip of your tongue.

3 Roll your tongue up like a taco.

Done ☐

EARTH

What is the Earth trying to tell us?

LOL

Kids are laughter superstars, cracking up between three hundred and four hundred times every single day. Go you! Meanwhile, adults are a bit more chuckle challenged. They only laugh fifteen times a day.

Think you can get adults around you to say *HAHA*, *HEHE*, and *HOHO*?

Use your comedic powers to launch a family giggle extravaganza right now. Tell goofy jokes, make silly facial expressions, and share stories about your day. If all else fails, whip out your top-secret, never-before-seen dance moves. You'll be sure to turn any adult's frown upside down.

PROPER

Every proper person knows that the correct word is:

THINGAMABOB   **THINGAMAJIG**

Discuss why your version is correct, or at least the most fun to say!

68

HOMEMADE PIZZA

When my brother and I were kids, we decided to make the
world's most delicious pizza. We knew our
mom would be proud.

First, my brother and I mixed up an instant crust mix
from a box and spread the sauce on top.

I went to the fridge to get cheese. Uh-oh! We didn't have any
cheese. How could we be out? We looked everywhere.

It was time to get creative.

I can't recall what I put on my pizza or how my mom reacted.
All I remember is what my brother decided to put on his: a
giant carrot and a chocolate chip cookie.

What types of unusual toppings would you try on a pizza?

69

RELATED

You know our family is related because we all . . .

POT OF GOLD

Have you heard the leprechaun legend about gold? People say that there's a pot of gold waiting at the end of every rainbow. Imagine lugging home such an enormous treasure!

"How do you know the story is real?" my five-year-old asked.

I started explaining how most legends aren't true. They're old, traditional stories that people love to share to make everyday life more fun.

"That's not what I mean," he said. "What if people have been looking for the wrong thing? Not gold, Mommy. What if leprechauns hide something else at the end of the rainbow?"

I've been wondering if he might be right.

EVERYONE TRY THIS:

Grab a sheet of paper and draw a picture of what else a leprechaun might hide at the end of the rainbow.

TRUE TREASURE

When people think of gold, they often imagine power, wealth, and kings and queens. We have to be careful because sometimes we make gold feel so important that we forget the greatest treasures in our lives.

TALK ABOUT THIS:

What do you have that's more valuable than gold?

Done ☐

IT'S TRADITION

The traditions and holidays that matter to your family are special moments to look forward to. Some of your customs are celebrated by people all around you; some are unique to just your family. Part of what makes these rituals so special are the stories that surround them.

Ask an adult to tell you a story about a holiday or tradition your family honors.

MOO

Imagine you're a contented cow grazing in a field. Can you moo as you fill in this blank aloud?

TO-MOOOO-RROW
I WANT TOOOOOO
_____.

Who can keep a straight face as you doooooo this?

OBJECTS

What are three objects that your whole family uses every single day?

How smoothly would your day flow if one of them broke or got lost?

PERSPECTIVE SHIFT

You can always change your perspective.

When my husband, Martin, was a kid, he frequented a lot of art museums with his mom. She could study the same painting or sculpture for hours. Martin couldn't stand it! He had to sit and wait. And wait. He couldn't understand her art passion.

One afternoon while his mom examined a painting, he started daydreaming about something that brought him a lot of joy.

"I imagined that every painting I had to sit in front of was an airplane engine for me to study," he said. "Before long, I could stand there as long as my mom. I just thought about what I loved."

TALK ABOUT THIS:

How could you shift your mindset away from something you don't enjoy doing?

FRUIT

TRUE OR FALSE?

Fruit counts as a dessert.

LIVING ROOM

What's the most prominent thing in your living room?

PROMINENT
(prom-uh-nuhnt), *adjective*
standing out so as to be seen easily; most noticeable

TALK ABOUT THIS:

How do you and your family like to use this
important element of the room?

What does it say about the way your family
likes to spend time?

CHIPPED CUP

A teacup with a chip or crack is a cup with a story.

It's easy to feel like you're supposed to be perfect. You might even feel like other people are pushing you toward perfection. You try something, it doesn't come easy, and you quit. The next time, you don't even want to try. You're too afraid to take any kind of risk. You're too nervous to explore anything you're intrigued by. You don't want to experiment, even if it's something else you might love.

If your focus is on flawlessness, the spark that makes you so unique and awesome will start to fade. And maybe you will become just like those teacups. The flawless ones sit in the cupboard, rarely used for fear they might break.

But that cup with the chip or crack? Oh, it's got some great stories to tell! No one hesitates to grab it when they need a drink.

Everything about you that feels imperfect actually makes you stronger, wiser, and more interesting. Flaws are a huge part of what make you amazing just the way you are.

TALK ABOUT THIS:

Why do you think perfection is so important to people?

OLD STUFF

What is the oldest thing you're wearing right now?

Do you have any memories of when you got it
or when you wore it before?

TRUST

Just like a bridge, it takes time and hard work to build a
trusting relationship. When you use strong materials to
strengthen your bridge—such as keeping your promises,
helping out, being honest, and listening well—it can last your
whole life. You always have to be careful of adding unhelpful
things to your bridge. Actions such as using mean words,
treating someone unkindly, or harming someone's belongings
can put cracks in your bridge.

TALK ABOUT THIS:

Who are some people that you trust? Can they trust you too?

81

SEARCH FOR JOY

Give yourself a boost of cheer with this four- and five-letter word search. Link letters up, down, side to side, and diagonally. Each letter can be used only one time per word.

The words all relate to happiness. Spot JOY in the upper right to get started.

A	L	O	O
D	L	Y	J
E	G	I	S
E	R	M	N

(Psst. You might want to cover this part up. It's the list of words I hid. Maybe you can find more!)

JOY   SMILE   GRIN   JOLLY   GLEE   GLAD

Younger kids will love finding the letters one by one while you spell.

FOOTSTEPS

COUNT HOW MANY STEPS iT TAKES YOU TO WALK:

⭐ from the fridge to your bed

⭐ from the spot where you brush your teeth to your chair at the dinner table

⭐ from the front door to your favorite spot for books

⭐ from where you keep your shoes to where you keep your underwear

⭐ from the window with the best view to the washing machine

Which one took the most steps to get to?

Which was the quickest walk you took?

WORK IN PROGRESS

FiNiSH THiS SENTENCE ALOUD:

One really big thing I'm working on right now is . . .

SECRET DOOR

Picture this. You're lying in bed one afternoon, lazily looking around at the things on your walls, when you observe something you've never noticed before. You perk up, realizing that just a hop, skip, and a jump away from your pillow is a hidden door.

You climb out of bed and walk over to it. The door is pretty small. You squat down and reach for the knob. *Creak.* You slowly push the door open . . .

WOW!

Describe what you've discovered.

MASSAGE

The significance of touch is huge. It strengthens your bond with people, reduces your stress, and actually helps with your development—all without requiring any talking.

TRY THIS:

Ask your family if they'd like a massage. Is anyone open to a shoulder rub or some pats on the back? Are you?

YELLING

ARGH. When you feel a need to express frustration or anger, or when you believe your message isn't being heard, it's really easy to want to yell.

Does yelling at your family solve problems?

When someone in your family starts yelling at you, how do you feel? Does it make you do what they're wanting?

Brainstorm some better solutions than yelling.

87

HIGH FIVE

Give me five! Work together to name:

Five green vegetables

Five reasons to cry

Five verbs that start with s

Five odd numbers

Five European languages

88

PAJAMA PARTY

Discuss your dream pair of pajamas. Do they have spots?
Stripes? Cartoon characters? Long sleeves or short?
Matching or mismatched?

EVERYONE TRY THIS:

**On a shared piece of paper, take turns drawing yourself in
your dream pajamas.**

WORRY WEED

EGADS! A hideous weed has been growing from one of your worries. The more you think about what's bothering you, the bigger this worry plant grows. Can it be stopped?!

Do these four things to activate your 100 percent effective weed killer:

 1 Share your worry with your family.

2 Draw a really ugly weed on a piece of paper. This is your worry weed.

 3 Think of all the worry words and things that make your weed grow bigger. You can write them down beside your weed if you want.

 4 Discuss positive thoughts related to your worry. Are there things you could think or do differently so that your worry weed can't grow? Grab some scissors and chop pieces off your weed as you talk.

SPILLED MILK

My family seems to knock over a lot of milk glasses during dinner. (We're often distracted with the conversations you're sharing in this book!) We try not to get frustrated about the milk because you might know that old adage:

Don't cry over spilled milk.

This proverb means you shouldn't get upset about small things that have already happened. You can't change the past.

The only thing you can do is control your response and learn for the future. Mistakes happen! The milk can't go back in the cup. The clock can't rewind.

TALK ABOUT THIS:

Think of a mistake that happens often in your home.

How can you respond when you make the mistake?

How can you respond when someone else does?

NEW WORD

Why use boring old words to describe your day when you've got a word like ...

(kuh-KOF-uh-nee), *noun*

harsh and meaningless mixture of sounds

Things like morning traffic, a busy restaurant, or a classroom can have a lot of different sounds all happening at once, causing a lot of cacophony. Talk about any cacophony that you participated in today.

MUSIC MOOD

Music can be a way to express your emotions. Some songs make you sway and bounce, while others make you feel angry or sad. Great music is always good to have on hand.

EVERYONE, TALK ABOUT THIS:

What is a song that puts you in a good mood?

Done ☐

SLOW MOTION

ACT THIS OUT:

Your family is attending a local festival. You're dancing to the beat of the music, when something bizarre happens to the sound system. Everything on the loudspeakers seems to be playing in slooooooooow mooooooootion.

How do you look dancing and singing in slo-mo?

EAT O'CLOCK

What if you were in charge of deciding everything about tonight's dinner at home? *YUM!*

Think about what your delicious menu would include, where everyone would sit (are you going to the table?), and what you'd chat about while you eat. Just don't forget dessert!

STAND AND SIT

Give your hands a rest as you take on these challenges.

TRY THIS:

 Stand up from a sitting position without using your hands. Try it from a chair and from the floor.

 Remove your socks without using your hands.

 Balance a pencil on your upper lip.

Can you think of any other hands-free challenges to try?

96

PENGUIN PARADE

ACT THIS OUT:

Your family is a colony of debonair penguins. You're dressed to the nines in bowties and hats. You're carrying stylish canes in your flippers, waddle-dancing down the street.

What kind of music do you dance to during your penguin parade?

97

MOST LIKELY TO . . .

Name the person in your family who is most likely to . . .

fall asleep in the car
be the first person awake in the morning
stay up all night
misplace something they need every day
have a book in their hands
wrap you in a hug

98

INTERESTING ANSWERS

Conversations help you grow and understand the world in exciting ways. You never know what you might learn from a chat with a family friend. A teacher might share incredible new ideas. Your coach might have perspectives you've never considered. Even talking about random things with the people sitting around you right now can help your brain grow.

Here are some interesting answers. Can you imagine the conversations that came first?

 1 The last sentence is: *Oyasumi* (the Japanese word for "good night").

What was the conversation?

 2 The last sentence is: Save the cherry pie!

What was the conversation?

 3 The last sentence is: He's with a long-legged llama in Peru.

What was the conversation?

ADVICE FOR ADULTS

This question is just for kids:

What advice do you think adults need to hear these days?

~~~~~~

100

THIS FEELING

Our facial expressions and the way we use our bodies can tell people a lot about how we feel or what we think. Look around at your family right now. Notice how they're sitting. Do you see how their arms and shoulders demonstrate how they feel? What are their hands doing? Watch their eyes and mouths.

TRY THIS:

Give your best full-body expression for each of these feelings:

Hopeful   Cranky   Worried   Proud

Who makes some really great faces? Which emotion is most fun to act out?

OPERA SINGING

Instead of chatting today, try singing like opera stars as you all complete some of these sentences:

I am as quick as...

I am as happy as...

Our home is as loud as...

~~~~~~

FLYBY

What do you think this quote means?

"NO BIRD SOARS TOO HIGH IF HE SOARS WITH HIS OWN WINGS."

—WILLIAM BLAKE

HAIR DAY

Work together to give this family some interesting hairstyles.

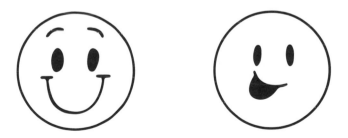

Discuss which ones you would try on your own head!

Done ☐

HAIR AFFAIR

Your hair is a tool you use to express something about who you are. It can communicate what you enjoy doing or a phase of life you're in. For example, the president of the United States has a different hairstyle than a world-class swimmer or a drummer in a rock band.

TALK ABOUT THIS:

How does your hair express something about who you are and what you like to do?

Done ☐

LAST NAME

Your last name is a piece of you that's really special. It connects you to your heritage, links you to your ancestors, and creates a strong sense of belonging among your family.

Do you know how your family got their last name?

ABRACADABRA

How would you rather spend the entire day?

Wearing shoes that make you leap like a kangaroo
or
Growing gills and dive underwater

Seeing your drawings come to life
or
Watching your toys come to life

Operating a homework-finishing robot
or
Running a bedroom-cleaning robot

It's time to open wide. How many teeth does everyone in your family have? Count them and compare.

108

FAMILY VACATION

Family vacations are dedicated time together when everyone breaks away from their usual routines to do activities they love and explore new things. The best part is your family can do things together. It might not always go as planned, but you can build an incredible collection of lifelong memories.

TALK ABOUT THIS:

What was the best family vacation ever?

109

SMELL THAT?

FINISH THESE SENTENCES ALOUD:

Ooooh, I love the smell of _____ !

*Eww. Gross. Gah! The smell
of _____ is the worst!*

110

SWEARING

TRUE OR FALSE?

Using curse words isn't a big deal.

Using curse words in our family isn't a big deal.

TALK ABOUT THIS:

Why do you think some people swear?
Why do you think some don't?

111

THAT'S BETTER

What always makes your day better?

MILK MUSTACHE

I mustache you three legen-dairy questions
that will milk you think.

 Should plant-based drinks such as oat milk
and almond milk be called "milk"?

 Which is the best way to enjoy ice cream:
lick it or use a spoon?

 Do berries taste better with whipped cream
or without?

COOKIE MONSTER

How many cookies do you think you could eat for dinner?

What type of cookie would you eat?

Why do you suppose only cookies for dinner
might be a bad idea?

114

WHO?

Name the person in your family who is most likely to . . .

take out the garbage

fix the Wi-Fi

start an impromptu dance

eat a lot of ketchup

take a nap

decorate the house for holidays

sleep in on Saturday

115

INSTEAD OF THIS

If you weren't working on this book,
what would you probably be doing right now?

Done ☐

116

ENGINEERING

Imagine you're a creative team of designers and engineers in a meeting. Your job is to design a dream vehicle for families just like yours.

What does this vehicle look like?

What does it need to be equipped with?

Is there some never-seen-before technology you could invent and include?

What doesn't this vehicle need?

Who in your family gets to drive it?

Done ☐

117

HOMEWORK

TRUE OR FALSE?

Homework is good for kids.

Try thinking of some pros and cons in your discussion.

EXTENDED FAMILY

Even though they can't always be with you as you work through this book, your extended family and close family friends play an incredible role in your family's life.

Ask an adult to tell you more about some of these people. Is there a specific person you'd like to learn about?

PETS

Many people call their animals "my best friend," and often for a good reason. Pets such as cats and dogs can be important members of many households, and they bring some people a lot of joy. They're also a big responsibility. In the United States, 66 percent of households own a pet.

TALK ABOUT THIS:

Should all families have a pet?
What if no families had pets?

HELP WANTED

Frog-some greetings, _____ Family!

I've got the sniffles because I'm probably the most unhoppy frog on the planet.

I heard about how you got out of a real pickle on #8. Un-frog-ettable!

Maybe you could help me out too.

You see, there are all these crazy old tales about what happens to people who kiss a frog like me. One legend says I'll transform into a handsome prince. Another claims you'll grow a bunch of nasty warts.

None of it is true! I'm not even interested in all that mushy kissing stuff. *BLECH!* I just want someone to play leapfrog with. Maybe we could try a few games of Catch the Fly or dance the Lily Pad Hop.

Please help! How do you make friends?

Your froggy wannabe friend,
TAD

OUR FUTURE

Imagine your family gets to fast-forward in time ten years. You'll get to peek at your bedrooms and the books that you'll read. You'll see how much taller you will be and the hobbies you will love. You'll even get a sneak peek at what's for dinner!

DAYDREAM ABOUT THIS, THEN DISCUSS:

What do you think your family's life will be like in ten years?

Done ☐

FUTURISTIC

HOLD ON! Before you can zip ten years into your family's future, you need a time machine that can get you there.

Grab a sheet of paper and invent a time machine that can carry your whole family. Then talk about this: What does it look like? What types of features does it need to include?

REBUS

A rebus is a fun puzzle made up of a combination of pictures, symbols, and letters. Can you and your family solve these?

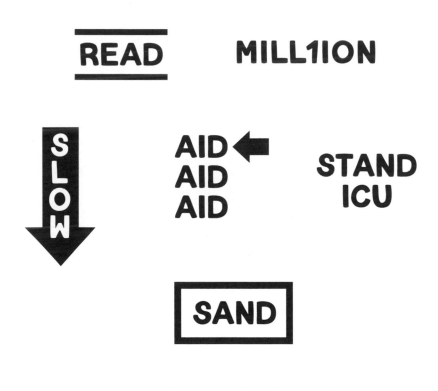

Answers: Read between the lines, One in a million,
Slow down, First aid, I see you understand, Sandbox

THE LOCALS

There is no other place in the entire world that's exactly like your community. Where you live is shaped by the people who live there today—like you! It's also influenced by geography, history, and culture.

In my hometown of Butte, Montana, we have some unique phrases that people like to say such as "J'eat yet?" and "How she goin'?" (They mean "Did you eat yet?" and "How are you?") The people of Butte have been greeting both strangers and friends this way for generations. It's a part of the community culture.

TALK ABOUT THIS:

What are some unique parts of your community's culture?

Can you think of any one-of-a-kind phrases that you hear where you live? Do you say them too?

125

FRIENDSHIP

FILL IN THE BLANKS ALOUD:

My best friend is _____,

and I love to _____

_____ with them.

126

WEEKLY TRADITION

Describe a special family tradition or ritual that your family does most weeks, such as a show you watch, a place you go, or a meal you share.

Why is this routine so meaningful to you?

What would your week feel like without it?

SURVEY

Get ready to raise your hand high (and see who else in your family does too). This survey is all about comparing and contrasting the little things that make the members of your family unique.

RAISE YOUR HAND iF . . .

you can ride a bike

you can't count to 100 yet

you have built a snowman

you can sleep in the car

you love chocolate

you wear glasses

you have slept in a tent

you like to touch worms

DILIGENCE

Sometimes it seems easier to ask someone else to solve your problems—then you don't have to solve them yourself!

My mom is an incredibly fast typist. Her fingers blur across the keyboard when she works. However, when I was a kid, I pecked my way through school reports, wishing she'd help me out.

Instead, she suggested, "Let's sign you up for a typing class."

Then I discovered that learning to type can be boring for a long, long time. You begin by placing your fingers on the keyboard and typing j j j j j j. Then f f f f f f. Eventually you start typing j f j f j f j f j. And you still have over one hundred keystrokes to go!

Wouldn't it be so much faster if we just had someone else do all the boring stuff for us while we go play?

The other option is to keep learning. Improvement can only come one step at a time. After a while, the obstacles get so easy you don't even have to think about them. Your fingers will blur across the keyboard too.

KEEP GOING

TALK ABOUT THIS:

Can you think of something that's difficult for you to do right now but is really easy for someone else in your family?

Can you think of something that's become so easy for you that you don't even have to think about it—like washing your hands or walking across the room?

Done ☐

129

NIGHT

Bedtime routines help family life run more smoothly at the end of the day. Everyone is exhausted, so having a procedure helps you know what to expect.

Discuss your bedtime routine. What do you like about it? Is there anything you wish you could change?

GLASSES

Perhaps people need more pizzazz in their pair of peepers, so let's do something about this!

TRY THIS:

Use a sheet of paper to draw the wackiest glasses you can imagine.

Now share your designs with each other. Would you wear any of these designs in public?

HERE'S A HUG

Give your family a few of these:

An awkward air hug
A sweep-you-off-your-feet hug
A surprise one-arm hug from the side
A big, warm bear hug

Which type of hug is your favorite today?

132

HEY, MACARONI

Every sophisticated person knows that the only way to eat macaroni and cheese is:

WITH A FORK   **WITH A SPOON**

Discuss your answer and why you chose it.

133

WOULD YOU

Talk about which you would choose to do:

THIS? OR THAT?

Travel to Mars	Live on the moon
Have a pocketful of endless snacks	Blow human-size bubble gum bubbles
Attend a school for superheroes	Attend a school for wizards and witches

Done ☐

134

FLIP A COIN

Brainstorm three situations where you might
want to flip a coin.

~~~~~~

Done ☐

135

The greatest measure of success isn't if you're the smartest or
the best. It's how much resilience you practice.

Resilience is:

- ☆ learning how to deal with disappointment
- ☆ taking on new challenges
- ☆ failing
- ☆ getting back up again, over and over

Ask an adult to tell you about something they competed in as
a kid—such as a sport, an extracurricular activity, or a school
subject—where they weren't the first-place winner. Does the
scoreboard matter to them today? How did participating in the
activity contribute to their life today?

HOME RUN!

Pretend you're a baseball player up to bat. You've got your eye on the ball, and you're ready to swing. Will you hit a home run?

FiNiSH THiS SENTENCE WHiLE YOU ACT OUT THE SCENE:

I love to snack on [whack] _____

GIANT STEPS

Let's wave my magic wand and—*SIM SALA BIM!*—you've just tripled in size.

How does being a giant make your life easier?

How does it make things more difficult?

When you're ready to return to your usual, perfect size, repeat the magic words: *SIM SALA BIM!*

MISS YOU

Missing someone you love is hard. You want to be with them, doing everyday things together. But you can't right now.

Who's someone you miss?

Swap some favorite memories and stories about this person.

STAND HERE

How long do you think you can stand on one foot?
Take a guess.

Now set a timer and see how many seconds you can . . .

1 balance on your right foot

2 balance on your left foot

Which foot was easier for you to balance on?

What about the rest of your family? Was that the easier foot for them too?

LAST NAME

Today's a great day to get your creative juices flowing.

Below is a list of categories. Your family's job is to come up with a word or phrase that fits each one. Every answer must begin with the first letter of your last name. (If the first letter of your last name feels too difficult—like Q or V—it's okay to use a different letter from your name.)

Are you ready to start the list?

A word that describes our family

Something we see at the playground

A dessert

Something in the fridge

A place to take a nap

Something with a tail

A crayon color

A mood

Done ☐

IS SOMEBODY?

Think of the people you see often but who aren't here with you now. Name one of those people who . . .

is taller than you

has the same hair color as you

is really good at saying *please* and *thank you*

can finish your sentences

shares a hobby or passion with you

makes you laugh

Done ☐

BOT FAMILY

ACT THIS OUT:

Oh dear. Your family is a bunch of cleaning robots that have started to malfunction. What's going on?! Try acting this scene out without touching a single object.

143

GOOD SENSE

You probably tell your family what you saw and did during the day. Not this time! Try thinking about your other senses.

♡ What's something you smelled today?

♡ What's something you tasted today?

♡ What's something you heard today?

144

BED BOAT

What if your bed were a boat?

Imagine the adventures you could take! You could sail through all kinds of waters. Maybe you'd embark on voyages all around the world or float close to home.

Tell the story of where you would go
and what you would see.

Done ☐

BREAKFAST

No matter what's for breakfast, a cup is probably sitting at your spot. What does it look like? What is it filled with? Talk about what it was full of this morning.

Done ☐

HAPPINESS

The ancient Greek philosopher Aristotle said:

"HAPPINESS DEPENDS UPON OURSELVES."

What do you think that means?

What makes you feel really happy today?

DANCE IT OUT

JUMP, JUMP, JUMP.

SHAKE, SHAKE, SHAKE.

You're in charge of inventing the world's next great dance craze. Show us your moves!

How does it feel to move your body in your very own style?

Then attempt your family's new moves too.

MARSUPIALS

Wouldn't it be handy to have giant pockets wherever you went? Your hands would always be free because you'd have a spot to stash everything. Marsupials, such as kangaroos and opossums, have built-in pouches on their bodies to carry their babies.

What would you carry in your giant pocket?

AROUND HERE

Stretch your fingers into the air. Now on a scale from 1-5, how awesome is your family? Five fingers for "We're the bomb-diggity!" Four, three, or two fingers if you're less fantastic. A single finger if your family is just ho hum.

Ready to try some more? Keep your fingers up.

ON A SCALE OF 1–5, OUR FAMILY . . .

likes spicy food

feels sleepy right now

enjoys traveling to new places

loves spending time in nature

is good with indoor plants

150

SOMETHING SPECIAL

You're fortunate to own so many wonderful things that bring you joy and help you grow. Do you know which one of your possessions means the most to you?

Do you remember how you got it?

151

THE CIRCUS

Last summer my parents were camping a couple hours' drive from home. I got this message:

"We're at the campground we stayed at two years before you were born. When they asked if we'd stayed here before, we said yes. We told them about a circus staying here at the same time. We remember looking out our tent and seeing elephants go by. We also heard the tigers at night!"

TALK ABOUT THIS:

What's a great story someone in your family has shared? Or can you think of one to share now?

HOT DOG

TRUE OR FALSE?

A hot dog is absolutely a type of sandwich.

TWIST YOUR WORDS

Tongue twisters are fun to say with your family because they challenge your mouth and mind, and they can crack you up. See how quickly you can say each of these:

Bob bakes big batches of bitter brown bread for breakfast.

Betty bought butter but the butter was bitter, so Betty bought better butter to make the bitter butter better.

Huh. She sees cheese trees.

Hold on. A happy hippo hopped and hiccuped!

Abe argues that apes hate grape cake.

AN OUT

Sometimes things go wrong and we can't fix them. That's why pilots always have something called "an out" when they're in the sky. They can't control unforeseen weather conditions, mechanical failures, or other emergency scenarios. But they can plan ahead. The "out" that they should always watch for is a safe place to make an emergency landing. Most importantly, they must recognize when it's time to stop pushing their airplane forward and get back on the ground.

TALK ABOUT IT:

What happens when you take on more than you can handle? What happens when you don't stop?

Done ☐

A FRIEND

What is the difference between being a friend to someone and being friendly to them?

156

THEY'RE AWESOME

List six incredible people who aren't here right now.

Discuss what makes each of them so wonderful.

157

SMILE

If you wanted to make almost everyone on the planet smile,
how would you do it?

OPPORTUNITY KNOCKS

Sometimes the opportunity to try something new
comes knocking at your door.

My six- and nine-year-olds just started taking golf lessons from
a neighbor. It's nothing formal. The neighbor just stopped by
one day and invited the boys along. Now they're learning the
proper stance, a little bit of swing mechanics,
and club selection.

They could have listed a hundred different reasons to say no
thank you to this experience. Instead, they said yes to learning
when an unexpected opportunity arrived.

TALK ABOUT THIS:

**What do you think happens when you give something new a
shot? What happens if you don't?**

IDEA EXAMINATION

Which is more fun for you?

TAKING THINGS APART **CREATING NEW THINGS**

Talk about your preference.

TRY THIS

You never know what types of secret talents you possess.
Give these challenges a try!

 Wiggle your ears.

 Raise one eyebrow.

 Rub your belly and pat your head at the same time.

 Make a fish face by sucking in your cheeks and pursing your lips.

What other secret talents do you have?

161

THE UNEXPECTED

Sometimes things don't go exactly the way you plan.

I remember one time we were supposed to have an epic snowstorm. My kids fell asleep with dreams of sipping hot chocolate in snow forts and launching an epic snowball fight the next morning.

But no one can predict the weather, and instead of snow, the temperature warmed just a few degrees and we got slammed with a never-ending rainstorm.

My grandma always used to say: "That's how it is, whether you like it or not. Pit pot."

TALK ABOUT THIS:

Why does it hurt so much when things you can't control go wrong?

Done ☐

NO SNOW

Luckily, when things don't go the way you plan,
you can still have a good time. The key is knowing
the one thing you can control:

Your response.

If you were expecting an incredible snowstorm and it didn't
end up happening, what could you do in the rain?
What could you do inside?

Done ☐

MOUTHFUL OF GUM

Picture yourself chomping on a massive wad of bubble gum.
NOM NOM NOM. Don't spit it out! Just finish saying
this sentence as you chew:

One thing I love about myself is

_____ .

164

HEAR THAT?

TAKE TURNS FINISHING THESE SENTENCES ALOUD:

AHHH, I feel so happy when I hear the

sound of _____ .

EGADS! I cannot stand the sound of _____ !

165

DINO DANCE

ACT THIS OUT TOGETHER:

Dinosaurs are roaming the planet again. Incredible!
This time, they're dancing too. Pick your favorite dinosaur,
then show your best dino moves in an impromptu
dino-stomp dance party.*

*Please don't chomp up the other dino dancers.

166

BREAKFAST

What's your preference for a weekend breakfast?

THIS? OR THAT?

Juice	Coffee
Pancakes	Toast
Leisurely	Quick
Lounging in pajamas	Being dressed for the day
Eating bright and early	Eating a late brunch
Staying at home	Going to a restaurant

CONSTANT

EVERYONE FINISH THIS SENTENCE:

Our family is always . . .

ON YOUR OWN

This one's just for the kids:

Is there something an adult does for you that you'd like to start doing for yourself?

169

WHILE OUTSIDE

Ask an adult to tell you a story about when you were younger.
The topic is you and an outdoor adventure.

170

WACKY SELFIE

Ooooh, boy. Celebrate your family's fabulous personalities with
a selfie shot that captures your life right now.

Try one of these kooky photo challenges. Or attempt them all!

♡ Everyone looking surprised

♡ Everyone striking yoga poses

♡ Everyone holding kitchen utensils

♡ Everyone holding something fuzzy

♡ Everyone touching their noses

Which photo is your favorite?
Do you know why you love it so much?

171

1, 2, 3

One thing our family always says is . . .

Two things our family is looking forward to are . . .

Three facts about our family are . . .

VEGGIES

Picture a massive pile of yucky vegetables on your dinner plate right now. You know, stuff like slimy brussel sprouts, asparagus, and spinach. Bleck! Apparently you're supposed to eat them all. Do you think you could horns woggle your way out of it?

HORNSWOGGLE

(HAWRN-swog-uhl), *verb*

to trick

Discuss your veggie-dodging, hornswoggling strategy.

COYOTE HOWLS

The first time I heard coyotes howl was a snowy February night when I was about eight years old. Dozens of my family members and I had gathered for a cross-country ski trip to an old, rustic cabin in the Montana wilderness for a three-day weekend.

"Mom," I nervously shout-whispered from my sleeping bag. "There are coyotes or something out there!"

"No," she whispered back from her sleeping bag, calming my racing thoughts. "That's your relatives."

One reason coyotes howl is to call their family—their pack—back together. Other times, they want to make themselves known to other packs.

The next morning, my cousins and I started howling together too.

TRY THIS:

Tip your head back and try howling like a pack of coyotes.

(Psst. It's perfectly normal to feel a bit uncomfortable at first. Relax and try whenever you're ready. You're surrounded by your people, your pack. Howling together is actually quite fun!)

174

SIGN YOUR NAME

Sign your name here. But hold on a second! You can't use your
hands to write. Put your pen between your toes.
Now challenge yourself to autograph this page.

Next grab a pen between your teeth. Carefully maneuver it to sign your name on this page.

Which was easier: writing with your toes or your teeth?

Is anyone's writing even legible?

FAMILECT

When you live with other people, you start creating your own unique words and phrases together. It's like a secret language! You invent inside jokes, funny phrases, new words, and special nicknames for each other that no one else knows.

This created language is called *familect*.

It's a type of communication that's an important part of your family's identity. When you hear these words, you might instantly relax. They make you feel a deeper bond. And they're a little reminder of how special your family is!

TALK ABOUT THiS:

Can you think of any special words and phrases that your family uses?

Share stories about how they became a part of your household language.

TEENY TINY

ALAKAZAM! You and your family just shrank to the size of itty-bitty ants. How does the world around you look now? Does anything look the same?

TRY THIS:

Lie on your belly and look around. Talk to each other in a teeny-tiny ant voice.

FRIDGE

I hate opening the fridge when—*PEE-EW!*—something has spoiled and the entire fridge stinks until someone identifies the decaying monster and gets. It. Out!

TAKE A GUESS:

What do you think the oldest food in your fridge is right now?

FORE EDGE

Writing on the fore edge of books is a tradition that dates as far back as the tenth century. Want to try it on this book?

The fore edge of your book is opposite the spine, the part of the book your fingers touch when you turn the page. Legend says that fore-edge painting first began when Charles II of England lent his books to a duchess who never returned them. The frustrated king decided he needed a secret book identification system, so he commissioned his court bookbinder, Samuel Mearne, and court painter, Sir Peter Lely, to devise a solution. Later, when the king was visiting the duchess, he pulled a book from her shelf—a book she had claimed was her own. With a sly grin, he fanned out the pages. And presto! Just inside the gilded fore edge was his royal coat of arms!

You don't have to make the fore edge of this book that fancy. You can just grab a permanent marker and doodle or write the year and your last name with a few fun words like

"THE CRAZY, COOL _____S!"

Discuss what you like most about your design.

(Psst. Want to see some of the fore edge designs my kids and I made? Once we used Morse Code! www.katieclemons.com/a/6pTV/)

THINKING CAP

Imagine you're a family of world-famous inventors. Someone frantically bangs at your front door.

"Help!" they cry. "It's urgent. I need you to invent me a thinking cap!"

You try to explain that there's no such thing as a thinking cap. It's a figure of speech that people say when it's time to think hard or creatively.

"No," they say, stomping their foot and refusing your explanation. "You have to invent a thinking cap for me right now!"

Hmm. You and your family need to start a brainstorm. Maybe you even want some paper to sketch some ideas.

What would a real thinking cap look like?

How would a person wear it?

How would it work?

1990S

Okay, kids, you get to answer all of these questions first. The 1990s might sound like forever ago, but to some people, it might feel like yesterday! If you don't know what something on this list is, make a guess! Then let the grown-ups have a turn.

How do you "talk to the hand"?
What is a collect call?
What is dial-up?
How do you use a fax machine?

TASTE THAT?

EVERYONE FINISH THESE SENTENCES ALOUD:

MMM. *I love the taste of* _____ *for dinner.*

BLECH! *There's nothing so gross as the taste of* _____ *for dinner.*

182

"GARBAGE"

We all love objects that other people think are unimportant. Some people will even tell you that the things you love are trash. They can't see the value that you see. They really don't understand the beauty or potential like you do.

Try not to let others decide what's good or bad for you. They can conclude what's right for themselves but not for you.

You get that choice.

Have the courage to keep loving your "garbage." It's part of what makes you such an incredible, interesting person.

TALK ABOUT THIS:

Can you think of a time when a person thought something you cared about was ridiculous?

How do you know that their opinion was wrong?

183

GOOD PERSON

FINISH THIS STATEMENT:

I'm a good person because ...

184

FAMILY HUDDLE

Huddle in a circle with your family. Now everyone, bring your hands together and stack them like pancakes. Stay that way while someone reads this aloud:

The hands you see are your home, and you can feel their strength. These are the hands that hold you close during challenging times. They cheer for you. They nudge you. These hands work together to build a future, to feed you, and to care for you. They are the hands that tenderly wipe your tears. They bravely lift you up. These are the hands that will always be there for high fives, endless support, and applause. They are the hands that love you. They are your family, your home.

LOVE YA!

It's official. There's no substitute for the words "I love you." You can try other phrases, like "I think you're awesome!" or "You're one cool cat." Those words make you smile. But they don't carry the really deep, warm and fuzzy, feel-good vibe you get when someone in your family says "I love you."

Some family psychologists even believe that the most important thing families can do is say "I love you" to each other every single day.

TRY THIS:

Look each person in the eye and tell them, "I love you."

Then look at them and listen as they tell you the same thing. Notice how you feel inside.

Done ☐

SUMMER DAY

Describe the perfect lazy summer day.

Done ☐

STREET LETTER

Help your brain grow by thinking outside of the box.

Find a word or phrase that fits each of the categories below. The challenge is that every answer must begin with the first letter of your street name. If you live on Gold Street, for example, your answers would all begin with the letter *G*. (If your street name begins with a difficult letter like *Q* or *V*, it's okay to pick a different letter, like the second or third one.)

Ready, set, go . . .

A thing that keeps us up at night
Something at a relative's house
Something in the ocean
A side dish
A boy's name
Something people are afraid of
Something with wheels
A breakfast food

SHOES

What's your go-to pair of shoes? Where do they take you almost every day?

~~~~~~

GREAT ADVENTURES

Recall some of your most memorable, most exciting family adventures. Think of day trips, vacations, visits with family and friends—it's all part of the wild ride.

 1 What's something that still cracks you up or makes you smile?

 2 Did you ever get stuck or lost?

 3 Do you remember spotting any animals or having a crazy encounter?

JUST EAT THIS

People love setting all kinds of food records—from the most hot dogs eaten at once to the biggest pizza ever made. Imagine you're about to compete in the world championship for the "I only eat one food" contest.

What food would you pick?

GREEN THINGS

Have you ever heard the phrase "green with envy"? The color green can represent jealousy, which is never a fun feeling. It can also mean new beginnings and growth, such as spring leaves and grass. Think about both of these meanings as you brainstorm green-colored things.

Which ones do you give a thumbs-up to?
Which ones get a thumbs-down?

SWIM

There's something about water that encourages you to wade, dive, or cannonball right in. The sensation relaxes your body. You dip a toe in. You glide. You splash and squeal.

Get ready to grab your swim stuff and imagine where you'd all love to go. Have each person circle their favorite water spot:

The ocean

A lake

An indoor pool

A natural hot spring

A splash park or splash pad

An outdoor pool

A creek or river

The bathtub

None—I'm more of a shore person

Discuss what you'd bring and what you'd do all day.
Just no sunburns, okay?

SWEET HOME

The community where you live contributes to the type of person you grow up to be. Some families live in the same area for generations. Others move once or twice, maybe even every few years.

How many generations of your family have lived in your community? Where did the first generation to move here come from? Why did they pick this place?

SOCKS

TRUE OR FALSE?

Wearing socks with your sandals is a completely acceptable thing to do.

Discuss why your answer is the most practical.

EARLY EATS

Ask an adult to tell you a story about
when you were younger. The topic is you and food.

196

RE-FORK

Silverware isn't just for eating! Some crafty people enjoy
repurposing vintage forks and spoons into household objects
and art. They bend them, weld them, and embellish them.

Brainstorm some interesting ways you could alter silverware
into something new.

YUMTASTIC

If you were a food critic, how would you describe the last meal you ate? Use silly, exaggerated words.

These phrases might help:

A FEAST OF EPIC PROPORTIONS

GOBBLE-UP GOOD

A TASTEBUD TEETER-TOTTER

A LITTLE MMM, A LOT MEH

NO SIGNS OF EXCESSIVE FIRE (I.E., IT'S NOT BURNED)

SCRUMPTIDDLYUMPTIOUS

STUFF-YOUR-FACE DELICIOUS

EH—A REAL FLAVOR FIZZLE

TAKE A SEAT

Exciting news! Imagine you've just won some incredible tickets. Your whole family gets to attend a live concert, performance, or sports game—whatever you want! What would you love to see?

Done ☐

SIT DOWN

"Wait, wait, wait!" a man is shouting in your direction. He's waving a few papers in his hand. They look like some tickets. Hang on, they're the tickets you just chose in the last conversation topic.

The man is gasping to catch his breath as he says, "I want to throw in something extra special for you. You get to pick tickets to see whatever you want. Now here are your options."

Which will you pick?

 Take the best seats and watch the event once.

 Pick mediocre seats and go to the event three times.

COUPONS

TALK ABOUT THIS:

Why do hugs from your family make you feel so good?

Sometimes you can get so distracted by everything happening in your life that you forget to lean in and give your family a warm squeeze. My kids and I invented a quick solution at our house: hug coupons! We just pass one to each other whenever we could use a quick snuggle.

Here is one example. You can copy and print this or make your own, or download infinitely more free hug coupons at www.katieclemons.com/a/bZBC/

THIS COUPON ENTITLES BEARER TO:

AN INCREDIBLE HUG

Immediately redeemable from any nearby family member.

NO TALKING

Think of something you do every day, such as putting your clothes on or brushing your teeth, and prepare to tell your family all about it.

But wait! It's time for *THE NO TALKING CHALLENGE*. You can only communicate through gestures, facial expressions, and any nonverbal cues you can think of.

You'll be surprised by how much you can say without words.

Now act out a task you do each day. Can anyone guess what you're doing?

MONEY

TRUE OR FALSE?

Money makes you happier.

Explain your answer, and really listen to what adults have to say.

POWER OF THREE

The number three has always had a unique significance to people. The ancient Greek philosopher Pythagoras considered it the perfect number. (If you haven't already, you'll learn about the Pythagorean theorem one day. It's a handy math formula for calculating sides and angles of a triangle.)

Don't sweat, though. We're not doing math right now! Have a little buzz session with your family. (That means a brainstorm.)

See if you can create these lists of three:

Name three foods that come in a can.

Name three rivers.

Name three colors that aren't very pretty.

Name three types of shoes.

MOPPING

No one likes making mistakes, even though they're one of our greatest opportunities to learn.

I decided to surprise my mom one day when I was seven years old. I'd seen her mop the kitchen countless times. How hard could it be?

I filled the bucket with hot water and dunked the mop in. Then I grabbed the dish soap and squirted half the bottle all over the floor. What a fun job!

That day I learned that we use different soaps for different jobs. Uh-oh. The kitchen floor turned into something like a slippery sheet of ice. Soap was everywhere; I couldn't get it off. Bucket after bucket of water, I kept trying.

Then my mom got home . . . and almost slipped and fell!

NOW iT'S YOUR TURN:

Ask an adult to share a story about a time when they made a mistake. Listen to how they learned from the experience.

VOLCANO VOICE

Are you ready to speak like a volcano about to erupt?

First, you'll start speaking at a whisper, and then you'll get louder and louder with every word. On the last word, explode. *KABLOOEY!* Flail your arms in the air. Jump up and down and act a little crazy.

Then become completely silent and still. Settle back into your seat and watch how everyone reacts.

EVERYONE, TAKE TURNS WITH THIS PROMPT:

If I ate only one dessert for the rest of my life,

I'd pick _____ !

Done ☐

TOO OLD

What's something you think you're too old for but you still like anyway?

207

TIME WELL SPENT

Talk about how you would spend the entire day.

DOING THIS? OR DOING THAT?

Driving your own boat	Flying your own airplane
Eating all your food in popsicle form	Drinking all your meals from a straw
Speaking only in rhymes	Speaking only in song
Eating pizza with ice cream toppings	Eating ice cream with pizza toppings
Being a superhero and saving the day	Being a supervillain and wreaking havoc all day
Spreading your arms and flying	Becoming invisible

Which one would you drop everything to go do right now?

CONDIMENT

The one true condiment every hot dog should have is

KETCHUP   MUSTARD

Or is it something else? Or nothing at all?!

SIT DOWN

Consider all the places where you sit or lie down in your house.
Where would you find these?

 1. The comfiest place to relax and take it easy

 2. The strangest spot you've ever slept

 3. The ideal book-reading location

 4. The worst seat to watch a show/movie

 5. The coziest place to chat one-on-one with family

 6. The ultimate breakfast-enjoying spot

210

JOKESTER

Laughter helps your body relax. The best laughs are the ones you share with the people you care about.

I'm pulling these jokes out of my family vault for you. A lot of people call these "dad jokes," but they're actually all my sister's favorites.

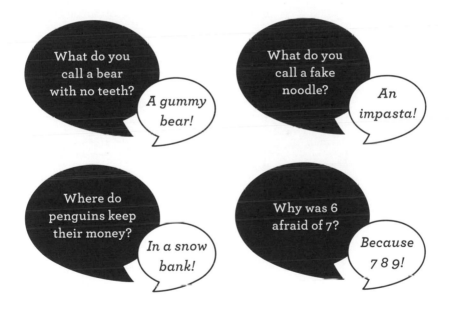

What do you call a bear with no teeth?

A gummy bear!

What do you call a fake noodle?

An impasta!

Where do penguins keep their money?

In a snow bank!

Why was 6 afraid of 7?

Because 7 8 9!

Do you have any good jokes you want to tell?

211

IT'S NOT A BOX

Do you see this picture right here? It's not a box. I know you think it looks like a box, but it's not.

Maybe it's a castle for crayons. A toy train bridge leading to the bookshelf. A secret cave for hibernating stuffed animals.

Or maybe it's something else!

What do you see?

CRACKS US UP

Chat about some of your all-time greatest inside jokes and crazy family memories.

DIFFERENT TASTES

Have you ever tried these foods? Would you eat any of them?

Pickled watermelon rind   Snails

Bubble gum ice cream   Fried pickles

Elk sausage   Kimchi

Shrimp and grits   Roadkill

Done ☐

214

HALFWAY MARK

"BELIEVE YOU CAN, AND YOU'RE HALFWAY THERE."
THEODORE ROOSEVELT

What do you think this quote means? Can you think of an example where this quote works in your own life?

Done ☐

215

SORRY

When you say sorry to someone, you take responsibility for your actions. You acknowledge, "Hey, I made a mistake." Your apology is really important for demonstrating that you care about other people and that you want to keep learning.

TALK ABOUT THIS:

Why does apologizing feel so difficult?
Do you think adults struggle with it too?

PLAYGROUND

The playgrounds in Berlin, Germany, receive a lot of praise for their unique and imaginative designs. Kids can pump spigots that take water down wooden channels and canals. They can climb aboard a ship to gaze through the telescope. They can shimmy up ladders to metal slides two stories high, grab an imaginary ice cream cone at the playhouse shop, or zip-line beneath the shade of linden trees. It's a wonderful, busy day for the kids of Berlin.

Imagine you're designing an incredible playground for your community. Here are a few things to consider:

1. What types of playground equipment would you include?

2. What would you add so that adults enjoy themselves?

3. What would you add to make your playground inclusive for kids of all abilities?

4. What types of natural elements would you incorporate, such as sand, boulders, water, trees, or other plants?

5. Will you include shops or other venues nearby?

6. What will you name your playground?

217

OUTSIDE AND INSIDE

Chat about things your family loves doing this time of year both inside and out. Then jot some down in these columns.

OUTSIDE	INSIDE

(Psst. Flip back to #26 to compare your current preferences with what you recorded when the season was different.)

Done ☐

218

I SEE

Ask an adult to answer this question:

What do you see when you look at me?

I SPY

Look left. Look right. Then look up and down. Maybe you need to twist around to see what's there. Now work with your family to spy these things around you. Can you find something:

Round	Red	Scratchy
Huge	Warm	Plastic
Old	Broken	Smooth

You can draw a picture of each item you find, or mark each square with a small object like a piece of cereal or paper clip. Can you get three in a row?

ACHIEVEMENTS

Here are three cheers for all of your incredible achievements.
HIP HIP HOORAY! HIP HIP HOORAY! HIP HIP HOORAY!

It can be easy for us to forget that there are so many little
things to celebrate, such as learning a new skill, achieving a
goal, or overcoming an obstacle.

My two-year-old just climbed up the tree fort at the playground
all by herself. Sure, the big kids have been doing this for years.
But not her. "Bravo!" she cheered from the top,
clapping and clapping.

Beat the drum and blow the horn. It's time to celebrate you!
What's a recent achievement or milestone
you're proud of reaching?

SNACK DISPENSER

If you had a built-in snack dispenser at home, what would you
fill it with? How would it work?

CAST A VOTE

You are meant to be uniquely you.

What if everyone always had exactly the same ideas as you? Or they all wore their hair the same way? Or everyone ate the same foods and had the same hobbies? Which parts of yourself would you have to abandon so you could be identical to everyone else?

Now imagine you felt really strongly about something but your opinion didn't match everyone's around you.

Jeannette Rankin believed in the power of nonviolence and the importance of promoting peace to resolve conflict. She was the first female to serve in the United States Congress in 1916. The next year, she courageously cast her vote against the United States' entry into World War I along with other members of Congress. People everywhere started to criticize her.

Fast-forward to 1940. She was reelected to Congress, and it was time to decide if the US should enter World War II. Again, Jeannette voted no. This time she was the only person.

TALK ABOUT IT:

What's something you're really passionate about? Would you stand up for it if you were the only one?

FUNNY FLAMINGOS

ACT THiS OUT:

Oh, wow! Your family is a flock of flamingos doing a synchronized dance routine with lots of leg kicks. Is it beautiful? Is it leggy and awkward? Do you squawk or talk as you dance? Stand up and let's find out!

MAGIC LEVER

If this giant lever were a magic switch that would do something ridiculous when pulled, what would it do? Would you pull it?

HOMEWARD

Imagine you're moving to someplace completely new to your family. Chat about which one you'd rather call home.

THIS? OR THAT?

Jungle	Desert
Ocean	Mountains
Country	City
A place with snow	A place with palm trees

PARROT TALK

Parrots are vocal learners, which means they understand sounds by hearing them and then mimicking them. They'll imitate anything from creaking doors to barking dogs. They'll even repeat phrases they learn from their owners.

If you had a pet parrot, what would you teach it to say?

FOREIGN LANGUAGE

If you could snap your fingers and become fluent in any language, which language would you choose? What would you do with your new skill?

HELIUM HEAD

Picture this: You just grabbed hold of a giant balloon floating through the air. You inhale its helium and—what's this?—your voice transforms into a whimsical, high-pitched chipmunk sound. Use your helium-head voice to recite this famous phrase aloud:

Whatever you are, be a good one.

229

KINDNESS CLUES

Kindness is contagious. When you consistently practice kindness, you feel the positive change you're making in the world. The people that you're kind to and the people who witness it feel happier too.

This game is an easy way to reflect on kind gestures. Did you or your family do one of these things today? Cross it off or put an object—such as a coin or candy—on each one! See if you can get three in a row.

Held the door for someone	Made someone feel welcome	Did an unexpected chore
Made someone laugh	♡	Apologized
Complimented someone	Said, "I love you"	Read to someone

Done ☐

KNOWLEDGE

FiNiSH THiS SENTENCE:

One thing I'd love to learn how to do is . . .

〜〜〜〜〜〜〜〜〜〜〜〜〜〜〜〜〜

Done ☐

231

MODERN CONVENIENCE

It wasn't that long ago that kids like you were riding horses to school. My grandpa lived on a ranch in rural Montana in the 1920s. If he wanted to attend school in town, he had to ride his horse. Back then, families didn't always have toilets in their houses, or cars to get where they needed to go. They managed without many of the comforts we love today.

Pick which convenience you'd be most willing to give up:

Indoor plumbing   Cars

Internet   Refrigerators

Done ☐

ORGANIZER

What's something you like to keep organized?

What's something you're not so good at keeping tidy?

Done ☐

SATURDAY

TRUE OR FALSE?

Saturday is the best day of the week.

Why do you say that?

What would you like to do this weekend?

FIRST TIME

Trying new things that aren't familiar to you can feel really scary.
Often, it can also be really rewarding! Talk about the last time
you did something new. It can be something
huge or something small.

FRUITY

Did you know that cranberries can bounce? (I'm not sure if you're
supposed to test this inside your home!) Here's another fruit
fact: Did you know that strawberries are technically not berries?
Strawberries have seeds on the outside, while berries
have seeds on the inside.

TALK ABOUT IT:

**If you could grow any type of fruit at home year round,
what kind would you pick?**

YUM! **Why did you choose the fruit you did?**

MATCHING T-SHIRTS

Well, look at that. Your family is about to own matching T-shirts! Chat about what you'd like it to look like.

Who do you think would be the most excited to wear this shirt?

Who would not be so thrilled to wear it?

WORKING

What do you think is the best job in the entire world?

What do you think is the most difficult job?

What do you think is one of the most important jobs?

WITH A HUG

TRY THESE:

An awww-how-nice-to-see-you-again hug

A hug with T. rex arms

A hug with a kiss on each cheek

An "I love you soooo much" hug

Which hug felt like the best one today? Can you think of
a time when another hug might feel better?

PLACES

Where are three places in your community that your family goes to a lot?

Go through these questions for each location:

♡ How do you get there?

♡ Why do you go there?

♡ Do you like going there?

PIZZA

TRUE OR FALSE?

Pineapple does not belong on pizza. *Ever!*

 **241**

OVER TIME

Sometimes your days might feel very similar to each other. But little by little, you are growing and changing. It's easy to spot these changes in the seasons. Winter is very different than summer! But it's trickier to see the change happening in yourself.

TALK ABOUT iT:

Where were you one year ago?

Where were you five years ago?

Where were the adults with you twenty years ago?

How about thirty years ago?

242

SPORTS FAN

Pretend you're watching your favorite sport.
GASP. GROAN. WHOOP. CHEER. CLAP. GRUNT.

Are you in the zone? When you are, take turns finishing this
sentence aloud with your best sports-fan voice:

I could eat _____ *and*

_____ *all day.*

243

BEEN THERE

The world has so many wonderful places to be.

How many states or countries has everyone in your
family visited? Tally them up!

Is there a state or country that you'd like to visit as a family?

CONNECTION

It's hard when someone you love can't be with you. Luckily, technology and good old-fashioned paper and pens have made connecting with loved ones really easy. They're not as powerful as your hugs, but they can still be effective.

First, think of someone you all love who's far away.
Who comes to mind?

Next, try one of these activities. Which sounds the most fun?

♡ Work as a family to write them a letter.

♡ Send them a drawing of an activity you enjoy doing with them.

♡ Take a family selfie and text it to them.

♡ Call them or do a video chat together.

♡ Find a special memento that they've given to you and use it or wear it.

♡ Send them a song they love (you could even send them a ten-second video of you dancing or singing along).

245

MAKER

What is one craft, recipe, or project that
you want to learn how to make?

~~~~~~

246

THIS OR THAT

Chat about what you'd rather do at home.

THIS? OR THAT?

Play a board game	Play a computer game
Make a craft project	Try a science experiment
Toss a ball together	Dance together
Do homework	Unload the dishwasher
Draw	Write

Can you come up with another "this or that" idea of your own?

247

GROW YOUR BRAIN

Sometimes making mistakes doesn't feel good. But guess what? Every time you do something incorrectly, an incredible spark lights in your brain. It figures out how to do better next time. Your error actually helps your brain grow.

The next time you make a mistake, think of it as an opportunity to learn more.

TALK ABOUT THIS:

Can you think of an example of a mistake you made today?

How do you think it helped your brain grow?

248

UPSIDE DOWN

Take a guess. Who in your family can do a headstand?

How about a handstand?

Now let's find out!

HIGH FIVE!

Read the list below aloud. Then raise your hand and give everyone in your family a high five each time something is true. You can even clap your own hands together to high five yourself!

 Our family takes care of each other.

 Our family works to be the best we can be.

 Our family keeps going, even when something feels hard.

 Our family is awesome.

BONES BREAK

Sometimes you've got to get hurt to truly appreciate how strong you are inside.

Have you ever broken a bone?

What do you remember about the recovery?

251

THEME PARK

Imagine your family owns their very own theme park. Families from around the world will come to witness the magic you make. What kind of wonders would you love to include? Jot down your wildest dreams on a piece of paper.

Here are some categories you'll want to think about:

Must-try rides for all ages

Parades

Restaurants

Beloved characters

Shops

Shows

Done ☐

252

THEME PARK PLAN

Families are going to have so much fun visiting this marvelous world of whimsy that you just brainstormed!

 Decide on an official park name.

 Draw a map for families to follow. Add some of your favorite brainstorm ideas, and don't forget bathrooms!

Done ☐

253

HAVE YOU EVER?

Wiggle your fingers and warm them up. Whenever you've done something on this list point at yourself and say, "That's me!" Swap stories as you go.

Sung songs around a campfire

Been to an old-fashioned candy store

Grown your own food

Gone rock climbing

Built a snowman

Skipped stones across a lake or river

Flown in a helicopter

Been in a parade

Ridden a city tour bus

(Psst. Identify one that you'd all like to do together one day.)

254

KEEP CREATIVE

There are over eight billion people on Earth. You will never be able to please them all. No one can!

You can draw an incredible picture that most people will love, but there will always be a few who won't like it. Maybe you write a funny story, invent something useful, or make a nature discovery. Not everyone will think it's great.

Sometimes those people will make sure you hear how bad they think it is. Don't waste your energy arguing with them or trying to prove them wrong.

Instead, concentrate on creating and discovering more wonderful things. Focus on the people who love what you're doing. And think about how happy you feel doing what you love.

TALK ABOUT THIS:

What's something unique that you enjoy doing? Why does it bring you so much joy?

FIRST LETTER

Look around at your crew and figure out whose birthday
is next on the calendar.

It's not time to blow out candles yet. Just grab the first letter of
their name. Next, as a family, come up with a word or phrase to
answer each prompt below. The challenge is that
every answer must begin with that letter.

Give these a try!

A girl's name (not the future birthday person's name)

Something our family does together

An action word (such as *run* or *shout*)

A snack

Something red

A bad habit

Something cold

Something you sit on

256

Done ☐

TOP TEN

List ten things that make your family feel happy:

1 This funny movie or show...

2 This informative book...

3 This really fat book...

4 This soothing song...

5 This old movie...

6 This kid's song...

7 This cartoon...

8 This picture-less book...

9 This famous song...

10 This holiday movie...

SLEEP BETTER

What's the most comfortable sleeping position of all time?
You might need to get on the ground and demonstrate it!
How do you usually sleep?

GOOD MORNING

Have you ever wondered what makes each day special? You
open your eyes to a world of possibilities when you wake up.
Rub the sleep out of your eyes if you need to. Maybe today's
the day you discover new skills, overcome challenges, or laugh
until your belly hurts. Or perhaps you'll do all of these things!

TALK ABOUT THIS:

What do you look forward to when you wake up?

WITH A TAIL

What would you do if you had a tail?

SUPERHERO

Attention all incredible superheroes! (That's you.) The time is here to rise up and strike the ultimate superhero pose. Have you got yours?

Now get ready to *POW! BAM!* and *ZOOM!* as you take turns knocking out this sentence with your most epic superhero voice:

The best part of being ＿＿ years old is

＿＿＿＿＿＿＿＿＿＿＿＿＿＿ !

SIMILE

As quickly as you can, read these phrases aloud and say the first thing that comes to mind. Make sure everyone gets the chance to contribute.

> ## OUR FAMILY IS . . .
>
> as quick as ...
>
> as happy as ...
>
> as busy as ...
>
> as loud as ...
>
> as slow as ...
>
> as wild as ...
>
> as helpful as ...
>
> as hungry as ...
>
> We are so _____ !

262

JOKE JAR

Sometimes we all just need a good laugh. That's why my family keeps a joke jar. It's just an old food container filled with jokes we've jotted down on slips of paper or printed off the internet.

When our conversation lags or we need to refocus (especially during dinner), we pull out a joke and read it aloud.

TO MAKE YOUR OWN JOKE JAR:

Grab a clean container, such as an empty yogurt bucket, a pickle jar, or a goofy mug from the back of the cabinet. Make a label like the one below, add your family's last name, and tape it to your container. Then fill it with your favorite laugh-out-loud jokes!

OUR FAMILY
JOKE JAR

EXPAND YOUR JOKE COLLECTION:

Get started with the jokes on #210. Or grab the ready-to-print collection of jokes that my kids and I put in our family's jar at www.katieclemons.com/a/hTkk/

PRICELESS

My family was driving home from ski club one Saturday evening when I spotted a giant billboard on the edge of town. It said:

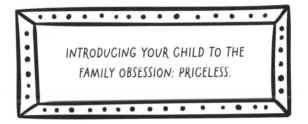

INTRODUCING YOUR CHILD TO THE FAMILY OBSESSION: PRICELESS.

We immediately knew what our family's weekend obsession was. What's yours?

TODAY'S SOMETHING

♡ What's something that you did with your hands today?

♡ What's something you sat on today that wasn't a chair?

♡ What's something blue that you touched today?

NOT TO-DO

The world is filled with to-do lists, telling us all the responsibilities we need to check off. Flip this idea upside down. What if your family made a NOT to-do list instead? A not-to-do list is your own unique list of tasks and habits that you should never do. It can help you stay focused on the important things and people in your life.

THE _____ FAMILY
NOT-TO-DO LIST

In our family, we do not ...

say...

laugh at...

forget...

eat...

leave without...

neglect...

266

TRIANGLE

Grab your own sheet of paper and draw a triangle on it.
Make your triangle any size and any angle.

Exchange triangle pictures with your family.

Now that you have a new piece of paper with a triangle, what
do you see? Is that triangle really a corn chip? a shark fin?
a roof? Finish the drawing, turning it into anything
you can imagine.

267

BEING CREATIVE

Ask an adult to tell you a story about when you were younger.

The topic is you and your creativity, such as a project you
made or activity you explored.

If you still have some time, ask them to tell you about a
creative interest they had as a kid. I'll bet they did
something pretty cool!

268

SOME HELP

If you could have a daily attendant come to your house for an hour a day, what would you have them do for you? You can be as lazy as you want during this imaginary hour.

Here are a few ideas:

Clean and do your chores

Cook your meals

Prep your snacks

Serve your meals and snacks

Give your personal care (such as filling your bathtub, styling your hair)

Run your errands

Maintain and repair (any broken toys?)

Assist with your social activities

Tutor you

Coach or instruct you

Chauffeur you

Done ☐

269

SICK

What makes you feel better when you're sick in bed?

Done ☐

270

MEET ME HERE

Just outside of the town of Webster, Massachusetts, is . . . take a long breath . . . Lake Chaubunagungamaug.

This lake has the longest name of any geographic feature in the United States. Some people just call it Webster Lake. Other people like to use its really long, exaggerated name that's forty-five letters long. Give pronouncing it a try:

LAKE CHARGOGGAGOGGMANCHAUGGAGOGGCHAUBUNAGUNGAMAUGG

Whew! Why do you think preserving such a unique name might be important to the people who live there today?

Do you know how your community got its name?

271

HIDDEN

How lucky are you?! Imagine you've got a chest filled with treasure. What would be inside? Where would you bury it?

272

ANTS IN MY PANTS

Ants are tricky to corral. They climb all over anything (or anyone) that's interfering with their mission to collect food. Inevitably, more ants come along. Soon, they're all you can focus on.

Negative thoughts work the same way. One comes along, and then suddenly, they're everywhere! If you let them, they can distract you from everything else.

Just like ants, negative thoughts become the only thing you can think about.

TALK ABOUT THIS:

Can you think of a time when negative thoughts distracted you?

ANT JAR

YAHOO! I don't know how you did it, but you caught all of those pesky ants and their negative thoughts, and you stuck them in a jar.

Now that they can't distract you, enjoy focusing on positive thoughts that make you smile.

TRY THIS:

List some details you love about yourself, such as . . .

your strengths   your creative ideas

your kindness   your determination

TIME TO EAT

MMM. "Dinnertime!" One of life's greatest words.
I imagine you usually walk to the table. Sometimes when
you're really hungry, you might run.

Not this time!

ACT THiS OUT:

Have a family member yell out, "Dinnertime!"
Then instead of walking or running, pick one of
the words below and approach the table.

CRAWL	MOONWALK
SNEAK	STROLL
SKIP	LEAP
FLUTTER	TIPTOE

LOVE ATTACK

Families often have one adult who doesn't make it into many photos. They're busy taking the pictures and juggling everyone's needs, or they don't feel comfortable hopping into the frame.

Is there an adult in your group that you could really shower with all your big, slobbery kisses and warm bear hugs right now?

Take a group selfie of your gentle love attack on this person so that you can give them a photo treat they'll treasure.

MUSIC

What if you were required to listen to only one singer or band for the rest of your life?

Who would you choose? Can you guess who everyone else in your family would pick?

IMAGINE IF

Your imagination can transform ordinary days into extraordinary adventures! Chat about what you'd rather do.

THIS? OR THAT?

Own a magic carpet	Own a time machine
Fly your own helicopter	Drive your own submarine
Sneeze confetti	Burp bubbles
Own a pet dinosaur	Own a pet dragon

Imagine another "this or that" idea to try.

BRRR

278

Describe why you give winter a thumbs-up or a thumbs-down.

DINNER GUESTS

If you could swap places with any animal for a day,
which type would you choose?

How do you think they'd handle eating your dinner?

ROAD SIGNS

If you could invent a wacky road sign telling drivers
what to do, what would it say?

BRAINPOWER

Activities that help you improve your memory and concentration are important at any age. Really stretch your brain today with this missing-object challenge.

HERE'S HOW TO PLAY:

1. Gather six kids' books.

2. Spread them across the table so everyone can see the covers.

3. Set a timer for fifteen seconds. Try to memorize the books in front of you.

4. Have an adult take the books out of the room, secretly mixing them up and removing one from the pile.

5. The adult returns and spreads the books across the table.

6. Can you recall the missing title?

GIVE YOURSELF MORE CHALLENGES:

Try this game with more books or a different genre from an adult's collection. The more you play, the better your brain becomes at finding the answers.

THUMBS-UP

Go through this list and hold out your hand. Do you give each
of these a thumbs-up or a thumbs-down?

I eat chocolate chip cookies.

My bedroom is clean.

Sometimes I jump on the bed.

I brushed my teeth this morning.

I like to eat spinach.

I make people happy.

283

ONE MILLION

YIPPEE! Everyone in your family just won a million bucks.
Take turns using exactly five words to describe how you
want to use your million.

ALL NEW

WOWZERS! Progress is here, my friend. Everyone's scooping up this newfangled kitchen gadget that makes family life so much easier.

You've heard other kids talking about how incredible it is. Adults can't stop gushing about how much time it's saving them. OOOOOOH GOSH, is it amazing! This lifesaver is about the size of a microwave and has to be plugged in.

Your family already ordered yours. It arrives on Friday.

The question is . . . *what is this thing?*

Use your imagination to determine what this new appliance could be. Name it too!

NO ROOM

OH DEAR. Your whole family has been so eager to get your hands on this all-new, must-have device that goes in your kitchen. You know it's going to revolutionize your life.

There's only one problem! Imagine you have nowhere to put it in the kitchen. One major appliance has to go. Which one could your family live without?

Dishwasher   Oven

Microwave   Freezer

Fridge   Toaster

WITH YOU

Ask an adult to answer this question:

What are some of your favorite parts of being in our family?

Then share some parts that you love too.

287

FAIRY GODMOTHER

Imagine fluttering through the world, spreading enchantment
and magic wherever you go. You'd wave your wand
or sprinkle your stardust and—*ZIPPITY-ZAP!*—everyone's
dreams would come true.

You'd spread joy. You'd turn pumpkins into carriages and mice
into elegant horses. You'd gift self-confidence, spread laughter,
and bring a feeling of hope.

Picture a special person in your life that you would
enjoy granting a magical wish for.

What would you love to give them?

288

FILL IN THE BLANK

FINISH THIS SENTENCE ALOUD:

I don't like to clean the _____ *because*

_____ .

IDIOMS

Idioms are illogical-sounding phrases that people say all the time. When you use an idiom, you say one thing, but you really mean something else. Here's an example:

IT'S RAINING CATS AND DOGS!

You know cats and dogs aren't falling from the sky. People just say that when it's raining really hard.

See if you can match these idioms with their actual meanings. Then use a few to describe your day.

I work like a dog.

I can't sit still.

I'm a fish out of water.

I'm similar to a parent or specific adult.

I'm all ears.

I work really hard.

I have ants in my pants.

I'm in a new or uncomfortable situation.

I'm a chip off the old block.

I'm eager to hear what someone has to say.

Over the next day or so, listen to the way your family speaks. Maybe you'll hear other idioms!

290

SCAVENGER HUNT

It's easy to think that snapping selfies is only worthwhile when you're doing something extremely unique or beautiful. That's not true at all! Selfies can help you capture ordinary moments too. They create a visual diary that's both fun to make and wonderful to look back on.

Squeeze your whole family into a selfie today, and showcase your collective sense of humor or your greatest attempts at seriousness with one of these photo ideas:

- ♡ Posing for a toothpaste advertisement
- ♡ Standing with a street sign
- ♡ Sitting in the car
- ♡ Doing a crazy dance trend
- ♡ Posing mid-bite

Discuss which selfie is your favorite and why.

291

CHALLENGING

Are you up for a few challenges today? I've got just the ticket to test your balance:

 1 Walk backward in a straight line.

 2 Balance a spoon on your nose.

 3 Balance an object—such as a nut or strawberry—on the tip of your finger.

What's another challenge you can come up with for your family to try?

292

WITH WINGS

What would you do if you had wings?

SCALE

On a scale of 1-5, how wonderful would you say your family is? Go ahead and hold up your fingers. Five means "stupendous!" and fewer fingers mean less and less incredible, until you get to one finger, which I'm sorry to say means your family is quite unimpressive.

Let's see where else your family stands.

ON A SCALE OF 1-5 . . .

We could eat more pizza.

We like reading books.

We recycle.

We're pro mess makers.

We love binge-watching movies and show

We enjoy bike riding together.

294

FRIENDS

When you have two or more people together, though, there's plenty that you can't control. What you can do is decide what type of friend you want to be and know what is and isn't okay to you. Read through this list and discuss what's in your control and what isn't.

I can control . . .

the choices I make

the choices my friends make

how I react when other people have ideas that are different than mine

how I react when someone else says no

how my friends feel

how I react when I don't agree

the way I treat my friends

how I listen

what my friends like and don't like

the boundaries I set

whether or not others apologize

how I apologize

COTTON CANDY

"THE IMPORTANT THING IS NOT TO STOP QUESTIONING."

ALBERT EINSTEIN

Here are some answers. Your job is to imagine the questions that lead to them.

1 The answer is: cotton candy (or candy floss).

What's the question?

2 The answer is: a piece of tape.

What's the question?

3 The answer is: a purple-and-gold rocket ship.

What's the question?

MEETING YOU

The greatest feeling in the entire world happens only a few times in your life.

On the day it happens, your body experiences an intense combination of nervousness and joy. The feeling keeps building because you know something incredible is about to happen:

You're going to meet a new person who you will love forever.

Maybe you're meeting a new sibling, your own child, or another family member.

Ask an adult or older sibling to describe how they felt on the day they met you.

Done ☐

MADE ME SMILE

Can you think of someone who made you smile today? Describe what they did.

298

HAVE YOU?

"LIFE IS AN ADVENTURE, A SERIES OF STORIES TO BE LIVED AND TOLD."

RALPH WALDO EMERSON

You have the opportunity every day to chase dreams, overcome obstacles, and try new things. Some of those things will be memories you will never forget.

Give a big thumbs up for everything that you have done. When someone else has a thumbs up, listen to their stories. You might hear some wild adventures along the way.

One of us has . . .

met someone famous

caught a fish

played in a band

learned to tie knots

won a trophy

helped raise money for charity

attended summer camp

CRACK A SMILE

How long can you keep a straight face? I'll bet you burst into laughter faster than you think, so let's find out!

Here are the rules:

1 Pick a partner and face them.

2 Be very, very serious.

3 Stare at their eyes and nose.

4 You can blink, but you cannot smile.

HOME

Ask an adult to answer these questions:

Will you tell me about a home you grew up in?

What did your bedroom look like?

What did your family do inside? How about outside?

301

THE ZIPPER ZOOM ZOO

Dear _____ Family,

After sixty-three wonderful years of operating The Zipper Zoom Zoo in a land very far away and also surprisingly close to where you live, it's time for us to close down the zoo.

Not to fret, my dears. Here's the exciting part: before I can close the gate one last time, my animals all need new homes.

Have you ever wondered what it would be like to have a pet like a hippopotamus or chimpanzee? Wonder no more. Your family is about to experience a unique, once-in-a-lifetime opportunity. I want to gift you one of my zoo animals.

That's right. Choose any animal you want for a pet! Talk among yourselves, and let me know.

Which zoo animal would your family want to care for?

Warm wishes,

MS. ZOOEY ZOOGLER, Owner of The Zipper Zoom Zoo

KEEP GOING

THEN TALK ABOUT THIS:

Pretending to bring home a zoo animal might sound like a wild adventure! The reality is that many animals probably don't make very good pets. Why do you think that is?

Done ☐

302

PARTY

YIPPEE! Decide what you'd like to celebrate today.

303

WORRY MONSTER

WOWZERS. This monster is insatiably hungry! He scarfed down a box of cookies. He popped all those socks missing their partners into his mouth. Then he devoured all the leftovers in the fridge, including the one growing fuzz behind the pickle jar. He wants more.

You know how your worries can eat away at you sometimes?

What if you fed them all to this adorable fella? Put your worries in his mouth, and I bet he'll gobble up every one.

Talk to your family about your worries as you feed him. You'll find that saying your worries aloud and redirecting them can make them feel small. They may even vanish.

GRATITUDE TREE

Being truly grateful to someone is much more than saying a quick thanks as you dash out the door.

You have so many wonderful people in your life. It's really easy to forget or neglect them. Practice recognizing the people you're grateful for as you discuss these questions:

Who's someone younger than you that you're grateful for? Can you think of a way that you could be more like that person?

Do you have a favorite family activity that always brings you joy? Why does doing it with your family mean so much?

If you could give a thank you award to someone right now, who would you choose?

(Psst. Take your gratitude conversation a step further and make a gratitude tree. Get the templates you'll need and all the instructions at www.katieclemons.com/a/ffzM/)

Done ☐

MONDAY

TRUE OR FALSE?

Monday is the easiest day of the week.

Why do you say that? How did your last Monday go?

~~~~~~

Done ☐

306

I'M TALKING

A chatterbox is a person who talks and talks. Day and night, they've got something to say. We can all turn into chatterboxes when we're discussing topics we're passionate about. It's fun to share facts and formulate opinions.

What's something you could talk about all day and night? You'd never get tired of this topic!

Why do you think you love this topic so much?

(Psst. If you aren't sure what you're a chatterbox about, ask your family. You probably have a topic that you talk a lot about without even realizing it!)

Done ☐

GO TEAM!

Imagine you're a team of football players. How do you stand? How do you sound when you speak? What kind of facial expressions do you make?

All right team, you're ready to read these sentences aloud with your best football player impressions:

Our family is . . .

We are . . .

And we . . .

Done ☐

308

TONGUE TWISTING

Ready to test your tongue-twisting talents?
Everyone, try to say these phrases aloud. They might
give your tongue quite the workout!

A NOISY NOISE ANNOYS AN OYSTER.

A SKUNK SAT ON A STUMP AND THUNK THE STUMP STUNK, BUT THE STUMP THUNK THE SKUNK STUNK.

ANY NOISE ANNOYS AN OYSTER, BUT A NOISY NOISE ANNOYS AN OYSTER MORE.

NO NEED TO LIGHT A NIGHTLIGHT ON A LIGHT NIGHT LIKE TONIGHT.

GAME

Sometimes if you gather around the table for a game, you create a strong sense of togetherness with your family, along with a bit of friendly competition!

What's your favorite board game?

What's your favorite card game?

ROAD TRIP

Pretend your famiy is heading out of town for the week.

Where would you love to go?

How will you get there?

What will you bring?

What will you do there?

TO-DO STUFF

Talk about what you'd rather do as a family.

THIS? OR THAT?

Perform in a theater   Watch a live show

Birdwatch   Stargaze

Rock climb   Golf

Jump on a trampoline   Have a squirt gun fight

Go for a family walk   Chat and share a snack

Of all these things, which sounds the most fun right now?

TOE TOUCHES

Can you touch your toes without bending your knees?

Try it standing, then try it sitting on the floor.

How can being flexible help you?

MEALS

You ask, "What's for dinner?"

You're happy when you hear . . .

You groan out loud when you hear . . .

BALANCING ACT

Steady now. Relax your body and keep calm as you attempt to perform these balancing acts:

 1 A spoon on your finger

 2 A pencil on a different finger

 3 A coin on the back of your hand. How about a stack of them?

 4 A feather (if you have one) on your arm so it won't float away

Who in your family seems to have the best knack for balancing small objects? Was one object easier than another for you?

Done ☐

TECH-NO-LOGY

Many adults worry about the negative impacts of technology. Today, try discussing all the positive things technology has brought into your family's life.

BRAVE

Sometimes brave can seem a bit boring. A brave person can have superpowers, a bright cape, and a huge spotlight to influence the world. But they don't need to.

The Wright brothers were American aviation pioneers who have been credited with creating and successfully flying the world's first motor-operated airplane in 1903. But they couldn't have done it without their younger sister, Katharine Wright. She was a vital part of their team . . . even if most of us have never heard of her.

Katharine was making a difference in her brothers' lives every time she lent them a hand, shared her ideas, or showed kindness. Once she even left her teaching job to nurse her brother back to health for seven weeks after a terrible plane wreck.

Her small acts of bravery helped give her brothers the opportunity to keep inventing airplanes and changing the world.

You never know how much you're changing the world when you act brave. I'll bet there have been many times when you've helped another person. Sometimes that's standing up for what's right or cheering someone on. It can be helping someone feel better or get something done.

Talk about a time when you felt like you made a difference in someone else's life.

SEASONS

AHH!

Think about your favorite drinks to sip or chug.
Then fill in these sentences aloud.

When it's cold outside, I like to sip a mug of _____ .

*Six months later, when it's really hot outside,
I grab a cold _____ to drink.*

318

TALKING VEGETABLES

ACT THiS OUT:

You're a vegetable. You can talk. You can walk. Now you've got
to convince your family that you're the world's coolest veggie.

How are you going to achieve this?

319

PERFECT PLAYLIST

BOOM. THUMP. BOOM. THUMP.

I think I feel some really good music coming on. Can you feel it too? It's time to chat about some of your family's favorite songs. Maybe you even want to create your very own playlist of songs.

What's a song that makes you want to jump up
and dance or sing along?

What's a song someone in your family is
always singing aloud?

Can you think of a song that reminds you of a
particular place or time?

Is there a song you never grow tired of?

If your family had a theme song, what would it be?

THOUGHTS

We all have our own opinions about what's good and bad. Your unique perspective is really valuable. Sometimes the challenge is knowing when to share your opinion. For example, do you think the meal someone made you is gross? Do you believe someone's art project is strange? My sister-in-law always says:

> IF YOU HAVE A KIND THOUGHT, SHARE IT.
> IF YOU HAVE AN UNKIND THOUGHT,
> KEEP IT TO YOURSELF.

TALK ABOUT THIS:

Why do you think it's important to share kind thoughts?

Why is it better to keep unkind thoughts to yourself?

Done ☐

321

DOING STUFF

Work together to finish the thoughts below.

Currently, someone in our family is

making . . .

watching . . .

reading . . .

playing . . .

feeling . . .

planning . . .

loving . . .

Done ☐

322

KID SAYS

This finish-the-sentence exercise is just for kids:

You know you're in trouble when . . .

CIRCLES

Creativity is the ability to use your imagination to develop new ideas. The more you practice the skill, the more inventive you become. Have everyone take a turn looking at this circle. Maybe someone looks at it and sees a beach ball or a chocolate chip cookie. What do you see?

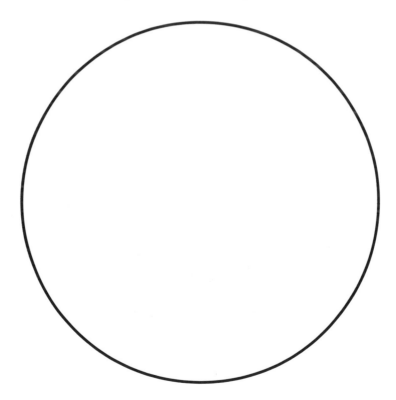

GRATEFUL

Our family is grateful because:

WE
ARE

WE
HAVE

WE
CAN

TOGETHERNESS

We all have people who are important to us, people who bring us joy and laughter and who make our hearts feel warm.

Who do you want to spend more time with?

PARAGLIDE

Have you ever spotted paragliders in the sky? To start their flight, a person either runs off a slope, such as a hill or a mountain, or they use a winch to pull them into the air. Meanwhile, their long, narrow parachute (called a wing) lifts into the air above them. Paraglider pilots can compete in long-distance races, perform aerial stunts, and discover all kinds of ways to test themselves in this sport.

But not today.

A professional paraglider has room in her schedule to give anyone in your family a free tandem ride. That means you'll fly together under her high-tech fabric wing made for two, each in your own comfortable fabric seat, for about fifteen to thirty minutes.

Who wants to try? Will you ask the pilot to perform acrobatic tricks with you?

WALK RIGHT IN

ACT THIS OUT:

On ordinary days, you probably walk into various rooms of your house. Luckily, today is not an ordinary day. It's Enter Rooms in a Different Way Day. Walking just isn't allowed.

Exit the room or space you're in. Instead of walking back in, try a few of these entrances:

STRUT

GLIDE

SOMERSAULT

MEANDER

SCURRY

MARCH

SLOG

ARMY CRAWL

Which style is your favorite?

328

FAMILY DEFINITION

What does being a family mean to you?

Do you think this acronym sums it up pretty well?

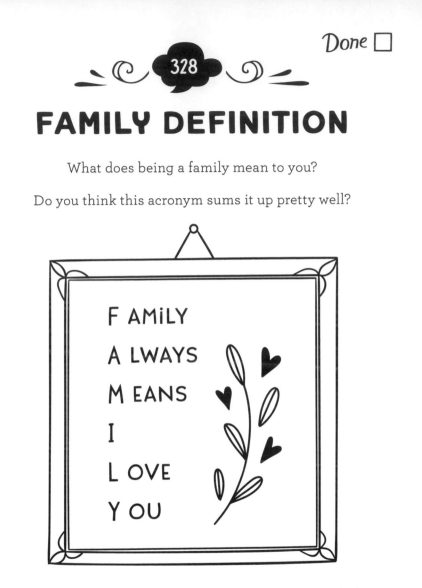

F AMiLY

A LWAYS

M EANS

I

L OVE

Y OU

(Psst. Grab a printable copy of this page to hang on your fridge, the front door, or anywhere you'll see the reminder. Go to www. katieclemons.com/a/ynBG/)

HAVE YOU?

You've done some pretty interesting things, and I'll bet you're not done yet. Read this list aloud. Nod your head up and down for every yes, and shake your head side to side for each no.

Have you ever . . .

sung karaoke

voted

been in a wedding (other than your own)

competed in a science fair

used a pottery wheel

had a penpal

given a speech

sold handmade crafts or food

Which one is something you'd enjoy doing again?

Are there any you'd like to try one day?

BLURP!

What is the funniest string of sounds you can make?
Who can keep a straight face when you make it?

Can you hold a blank expression when they make their sounds?

SPORTS TEAM

Which would you rather be?

The star player on a team that never wins

or

The worst player on a champion team

Now think deeply on this. If you were the star player, it might
bring you individual recognition and praise, but you might
miss the joy of teamwork and the motivation to grow. On the
other hand, being the worst player on a really successful team
might mean you face challenges and setbacks, though you'd
have an incredible opportunity to learn from your team.

RANDOM LETTER

At this point of the book, you've gotten the hang of brainstorming by alphabet letter. You've come up with so many creative (and sometimes silly!) ideas. Try one more!

Pick any letter of the alphabet today. Maybe it's the final letter of your last name, the first letter of your great-great-great-grandma's name, or one that's printed on the milk carton.

Now work together to find a word or phrase that answers each prompt below, beginning with your chosen letter.

Something you do at a party

A book title

A kitchen gadget

Something that keeps you warm

An object you might hide

Something sticky

An object you take on vacation

Something in the freezer

333

THERE'S SOMEONE

The people who help you are like sunshine in your life. They're the ones who make boo-boos feel better, lend a hand when things get tough, and offer a smile or hug to anyone in need. The kindness of their gestures demonstrates the power of compassion. They're proof that anyone can make a difference in the world, big or small.

TALK ABOUT THIS:

Who's someone who helped you today?
Why do you think they did it?

334

EAT LOCAL

The world is filled with countless foods that are specific to local regions and cultures. Talk about the foods that are very specific to where you live.

Do you like eating the local obsession?

TOY LIFE

What might happen if the toys in your home came to life?

YELLOW

Yellow is a cheerful color full of sunshine, optimism, and joy. Just seeing it can make people feel warm and hopeful.

1. Do you have any yellow clothing?

2. Are there any yellow foods you like to eat?

THE VENTRILOQUIST

A ventriloquist is a performer who can make it seem like their voice is coming from somewhere else, such as from the mouth of a puppet sitting on their lap. The key to "throwing your voice," as they call it, is two parts:

 Change your voice so it doesn't sound like you.

 Speak without moving your lips.

Talented ventriloquists give their puppets entirely unique personalities, which gets really fun.

EVERYONE, TRY THIS:

Grab a toy or object and see if you can use your ventriloquist skills to make it talk. Have it tell everyone about a chore you really dislike.

Take the challenge further and try having a conversation with it. Explain how you know this chore—as awful as it is—really helps your family.

HARD WORK

When Evelyn Cameron was growing up in the 1870s, she didn't even have to brush her hair. Servants did!

The easy life made Evelyn restless. She wanted to get her hands dirty, so she pioneered in the American West. She saw so much beauty in the untamed frontier, where she grew and preserved her own food, washed clothes by hand, and never had electricity to heat or light her home.

Then Evelyn began taking photographs: landscapes, cowboys, Native Americans, and the everyday activities of ranching communities around Terry, Montana. Today, her photographs are a priceless historical record of the spirit of the American West.

TALK ABOUT iT:

Which are you more drawn to: the easy life or the hard life?

POTATOES

There are over five thousand different types of potatoes and plenty of ways to eat them. Your spuds can be boiled, baked, or fried. They can be mashed, grated, chopped, or peeled.

What's your favorite way to eat potatoes?

What's a potato dish you love eating during a holiday?

MONKEY BUSINESS

ACT THIS OUT:

Boy, your family can sure be a barrel of monkeys. (That's a phrase you might use when you call something funny or amusing.) Except this time you're *actually* monkeys too. You're eating bananas, feeling curious, acting silly, and imitating each other. Goodness, what a crazy crew.

ASK QUESTIONS

The questions you ask can make a big difference in how you grow and learn. Curious questions might lead you to new and exciting discoveries about yourself and the world.
Imagine if someone asked you these questions.
Talk about what you'd say.

 Why do you think it's important to keep asking questions even when you believe you know a lot?

 Why do we need to keep learning when we can just go online for the answers?

WINTER SPORT

Which would you rather do?

Watch a winter sport

or

Do a winter sport

A WARM HUG

When you reach out to hug someone, a chemical called oxytocin kicks in to give you warm, fuzzy feelings inside.

Scientific studies have found that hugs can instantly boost your mood and help you resolve conflicts.
But you already knew deep inside how much a great hug means to you and your body.

Share a few of these with your family right now:

A back-patting hug

A pick-you-up or twirl-you-around hug

A crazy-fast hug

A warm hug

An emotional goodbye hug

A group hug

Which type of hug was your favorite?

LISTICLE

A listicle is a form of writing that's really easy to read because, well, it's a list. Grab a pen and write your family's listicle:

Kind things we can say to each other on a tough day:

(Psst. Make a copy of this page and hang it where you're sure to see it. Or take a pic on your phone and save it. You'll have it when you need to know just what to say.)

GINGERBREAD COOKIES

WHOA THERE, PARTNER! I don't want you chowing down on the delicious cookies just yet. First, you've got to gussy up these mighty fine gingerbread cookies.

Give them facial expressions to show how they really feel about your intentions to chomp them. Add some clothes and candy buttons if you'd like.

LOVING   EXCITED

CONFUSED

HAPPY

ANGRY

SCARED

When you're finished decorating, think about this:

Which cookie would you want to gobble up first?

Done ☐

COUNTDOWN

Count and see how many people in your family can do these different things. Raise your hand and speak up if you . . .

play an instrument
snort when you laugh
can make an origami bird
eat spicy food
feel comfortable touching a worm

Done ☐

SO PATIENT

Being patient is never easy, especially when you know exactly what you want. It's much easier to complain, get upset, or feel really annoyed when you have to wait for something.

TALK ABOUT THIS:

Why do you think patience is so important?

Can you think of something great that has happened because you were being patient?

348

WHAT IF?

When you use your imagination in unexpected ways, you stop doing ordinary things. You think of incredible new ideas that no one has ever thought before. Your creative thoughts might start small. But they can grow into wonderful discoveries.

See what kind of stories you can tell with these prompts:

> If my bottle of shampoo could talk, what would it be angry about?

> If our fridge could talk, what's the story it would tell me today?

> If the chair I sit on during dinner could laugh, what would it be cracking up about?

?!

HOPES AND DREAMS

Ask an adult to answer this question:

What are your hopes and dreams for me?

PEPPERMINT

My sister adores candy cane–flavored everything, so you have to watch out. She'll slip a few drops of peppermint extract into anything!

If you were in charge of your family's meals, what distinctive ingredient would you add to everything you eat?

351

BIRTHDAY

Imagine all but one of you are crouching in the living room. You're hiding behind anything you can find—chairs, toys, curtains... Shhh. You're waiting for that final member of your family to walk in. Streamers hang on the ceiling, and balloons lay on the floor. Oh! Everyone be quiet. They're about to enter. Take a deep breath. It's time to shout . . .

HAPPY BIRTHDAY!

Describe the birthday traditions your family celebrates.

Which tradition is your favorite?

Is there a special dessert you'd love to have on your upcoming birthday?

352

HOW DO YOU KNOW?

This question is especially for kids:

How do you know your family loves you so much?

MORE AND LESS

You are capable of amazing things. A lot can happen in a year. A lot just happened this year! It's all a part of learning and growing. When you and your family regularly pause to discuss what's working and what isn't, you will become more patient and understanding of each other. It's also a fun way to daydream and swap silly ideas.

Now think of the upcoming year. Chat about what you'd like to have more of—such as family pizza nights or time to chat about your day. Also examine what you'd like to have less of—such as spinach in your smoothies or how often you're running late.

Talk about why each of these things are important to you, and listen to how your family feels, too.

Just like you did in #6, you can grab a sheet of paper if you want. Then make a table like this one to jot down your ideas.

OVER THE NEXT YEAR, WE WANT:

MORE OF THIS	LESS OF THIS

354

WRITE YOUR NAME

Your signature is a personal stamp that marks where you've been and what you've done, symbolizing your unique identity. It also offers a powerful peek into how much you grow. Invite everyone in your family to grab a pen, then sign your names below.

Add your ages too!

(Hey, flip back to #1 to compare how much your penmanship has changed since you began this book.)

355

HOBBY LOVE

Hobbies are a fun way to explore what you love and try new things. Talk about which hobbies you'd rather do.

THIS? OR THAT?

Nap	Watch a bad movie
Bake cookies	Write code
Play chess	Play with clay
Play soccer	Swim
Read fiction	Read nonfiction
Take photographs	Scrapbook/collage
Listen to music	Play an instrument
Do a puzzle	Take care of an animal

Talk about how similar and different your family's preferences are.

BREAKING NEWS

It's time for a fun new way to tell your family about your day.

Choose someone in your family to transform into a sensational news reporter. Their mission is to interview you about your day. A whisk or their fist can become a makeshift microphone.

The first thing they need to do is barrage you with a lot of questions. They have to interview you about everything—from extraordinary events to ordinary moments that happened to you today.

Then they need to dig deeper for a good news story and reach out to other family members with questions like "Sir, can I get your opinion on the recent activity?"

It's like having a full-blown news network in your home, and you're the star of it all!

AND WE'RE LIVE IN 5 . . . 4 . . . 3 . . . 2 . . . 1 . . .

SHAPES

People say that beauty is in the eye of the beholder, which means that we all see the same things in different ways. What's beautiful to one person may not be to someone else. Look around you right now. You see a lot of different objects, right?

Look again. This time, pick just one object and examine the shapes it's made of. Maybe you've got a slice of watermelon. See how it's a wonky triangle? Or look at a door. Perhaps you can see a collection of rectangles.

Do you see how different the world can change when you look in a new way?

Talk about the other shapes that you can identify around you.

DO NOT PUSH!

There's only one thing you have to do today:

DO NOT PUSH THIS BUTTON.

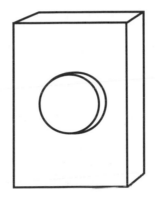

I'm serious. I know the button looks really fun. Your finger might be getting a little bit wiggly. But, seriously, don't think of pushing that button.

Do you know what will happen if you do?

ZZZ

Sleep is the most powerful reboot you can give your brain and muscles. Great rest helps you grow, learn, and be your best self so you're ready for another day of adventures and learning.

TALK ABOUT THIS:

What's something that helps you fall asleep at night?

What's something that startles you awake?

Done ☐

COLD

One of the drawbacks of winter can be the constant cold. Some people intentionally move to warmer places so they don't have to deal with icy windshields and snowy roads. Other people eagerly pile on layers of clothing. They've got skis, sleds, snowmobiles, or other equipment ready. Every family approaches winter differently.

What does your family do?

ROLL CALL

Have an adult pretend to take attendance like a teacher at school. As they list your name, don't answer, "Here!" Instead, respond with a wild animal sound.

When the next person is called, they repeat your animal sound. Then they add their own.

The next person repeats both sounds and adds one more. Go around and around as long as you want.

What a jungle!

WHILE PLAYING

Ask an adult to tell you a story about when you were younger.

The topic is you and a favorite toy.

Then ask them for a story about a childhood toy they loved.

NEVER CHANGE

You're reaching the end of this book. *BRAVO!*

What's something you hope never changes about the world?

What's something you hope never changes about your family?

ALMOST THE END

YAHOO! Throw some confetti and blow the horn. You've nearly reached the end of this book.

Can you recall a conversation that you really enjoyed?

What do you want to do with this book now?

What do you want to do together next?

365

LOVE IS

"LOVE iS THE BRiDGE BETWEEN YOU AND EVERYTHiNG."

RUMi

Rumi was a wise thirteenth-century Persian poet.

Why do you think he said this?

Do you think it's true for you and your family?

Dear caring adult,

BRAVO! You've reached the end of this book.

There are a lot of ways that you can change the world. Try them all! But also know that whether or not you can see it now, whether you ever notice, you have just impacted the world. You did it by slowing down and showing up to talk to your family over and over. When you think about the lessons and laughs you shared, you can see the ways you modeled kindness as you discussed each other's mistakes. You can recognize how you fostered a loving and supportive environment where you listened, told stories, cheered for victories, and comforted during struggles. You can chuckle about those moments when worries went away, and everyone just got goofy together.

Mother Teresa said, "Love begins at home, and it is not how much we do but how much love we put in the action that we do."

You just did that, five minutes at a time. All along, it was you nurturing this grassroots connection with your family. (It was never me or this book.) And believe me, with four kids at home, I know how exhausting and challenging it can feel just to get dinner on the table or everyone where they need to go, let alone launch engaging conversations! I also know how powerful it is for families to feel loved and listened to. The values that you modeled are already carrying over into your family's interactions with the world.

What a beautiful gift for your family. For all of us.

"Okay, now what?" my six-year-old, Linden, always asks whenever I finish reading aloud a big book.

Now I have a gift for you. If you'd like to keep receiving family storycatching ideas from me, get my free weekly printables and print-free activities. Families come for the unique and fun activities I share; they stay for something much bigger. I'll help you continue to nurture a consistent habit of connecting (and often cracking up, creating, and playing together) so that you can build the family bond you've always dreamed of.

https://katieclemons.com/a/cSqD/

Thank you for entrusting me and this book with your year of adventures! I believe that your story is one of the most meaningful gifts you can give yourself and the people you love.

Keep celebrating your story!

♡ Katie

KATIE CLEMONS

I'D REALLY LIKE TO THANK . . .

My folks. They taught me that I have a voice
and gave me the confidence to use it.

My husband. He knocks down my "I can't do that" walls
and steadies the ladder when I say "I can."

Friends like Talita, Christopher, Beth, and Michelle,
whose sentences often begin, "Katie, what if . . ."

Stacy, my kind and brilliant idea catcher and agent.

The Harper Celebrate crew. My gratitude as expressed by my
six-year-old: "It's soooooooooooooo big!"

Girl Scouts. Many mornings of wacky singing and evenings by
the campfire—the ripple effects are absolutely in these pages.

Teachers. I don't remember every teacher, and they don't all
remember me. Teachers don't have to in order to nurture
the spark in a child.

My kids. You will always have my cheers and love.
Keep being you.

Every family who picks up this book. Sometimes just a few
nudges can help to build the family bond you've always
wanted. I hope this book has done that.

Katie Clemons is a bestselling author and award-winning journal crafter of titles including *Between Mom and Me: A Mother and Son Journal* and *Love, Mom and Me: A Mother and Daughter Journal* and *My First Mom and Daughter Journal.* Through her guided journals and conversational prompts, she helps individuals and families celebrate their life stories and nurture deeper bonds while finding greater joy and gratitude. Katie and her storycatching books have been featured by media outlets such as *People*, CNN, the *Wall Street Journal*, *Huffington Post*, *Good Housekeeping*, and *Pregnancy and Newborn.* She is a fifth-generation Montanan.

Photo by MARTIN CLEMONS